French Wines

Tim Holland
and Arthur Bone

Macdonald Guidelines

Editorial Manager
Chester Fisher
Series Editor
Jim Miles
Editor
Alan Wakeford
Designer
Robert Wheeler
Picture Researcher
Jenny de Gex
Production
Penny Kitchenham

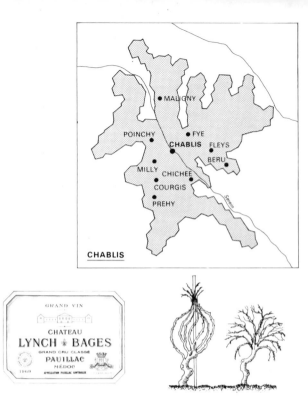

CHABLIS

Contents

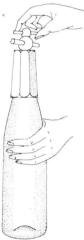

Information

Activities

Reference

© Macdonald Educational Ltd 1978

First published 1978
Macdonald Educational Ltd
Holywell House
Worship Street
London EC2A 2EN

Printed and bound by
Waterlow (Dunstable) Ltd

ISBN 0 356 06033 0

3

The reputation of French wines

France has the undisputed reputation for producing the world's finest wines ranging from the truly great wine to the good sound 'vin ordinaire'. For centuries now, these have graced the tables of France, and French history makes much of their prominence as gifts to visiting royalty and heads of state.

What other country can offer magnificent clarets, luscious Sauternes, great Burgundies both red and white, big heady Rhônes, succulent Alsatian wines and the sparkling gaiety of Champagne? And where else has nature provided man with unique conditions to match his skill? Soil, climate and a bewildering supply of suitable vine varieties complement the centuries of experience, expertise and dedication which have made the French vigneron the envied master of his craft. Throughout the world, wine growers have studied the techniques, imported the vine varieties, but few have even come close to the standard that they try to copy. However, their attempts have led to a general improvement in the style and standard of all wines.

The beautiful countryside of the vineyard areas, such as the Loire, make these ideal places in which to stay. In fact holidays in France have introduced many people to the delights of French wine, giving them the opportunity to sample wines not readily available elsewhere.

Quality—the key to trade

France can also boast that she has led the world in framing legislation to protect both wine grower and wine consumer. For example, in 1855, some Bordeaux wine merchants got together to classify some of their finest wines for the Paris Exhibition of that year. And in the 1930s the French Government set up an organization to protect and control the wine and guarantee names and origins.

Because of her geographical position, France has excellent trading relations with the wine markets in Europe, Britain and USA. Considerable though her exports might be, considerable also is her consumption. For example in 1976, for every person in the country, 143 bottles of wine were drunk. Naturally, the French prefer to drink their own wine, but they are not unaware of the fact that some drinkable wine is made in other countries. France as a result, is also a sizable importer of wine.

Struggle for success

Success for the French vignerons has not come easily. In the late 19th century, in line with the rest of Europe, their vineyards were devastated by an American burrowing louse called phylloxera, while during the present century two major wars have been fought on her soil ruining many of her vineyard areas. Prohibition in the USA and the depression in the 1930s also had damaging effects. And the flood of cheap wines from her former North African colonies hit particularly the home market.

Fortunately these problems have been surmounted. The drinking of wine is still an enlightened habit that people want to keep and one that is increasing not only in Europe but throughout the world.

▶ The traditional French wine-maker, the centrepiece of Renoir's painting 'Luncheon of the Boating Party'.

History of wine in France

The wild vine has been indigenous to Gaul, the old Roman name for France, since prehistoric times. Fossilized evidence found by geologists gives ample evidence of this. It was probably the Phoenician traders who first introduced cultivated vines into the south of France in about the 6th century BC. However, it is known with more certainty that later Greek colonists settled along the south coast and established trading posts. They sold both imported Greek wine and locally produced wine to the natives, bartering for boy slaves or other acceptable currency.

Wine was a very important commodity. It was not just another drink, but an important part of religious ritual as well as being used medicinally.

▼ The Romans played an important role in developing wine-making techniques in France. This mosaic shows a typical Roman vintage.

The Roman influence

It was the Romans, however, who had the greatest influence on French viticulture, with their superior knowledge of all agricultural matters. By 125 BC, they had established an important trading centre at Narbonne and from the Midi moved inland into what is now France. Wherever possible they followed the navigable rivers which gave them ease of transportation and a means of defending themselves against marauding tribes. As they radiated through the country, crops and vines were planted and the local people taught how to cultivate them. A setback to this development occurred in 92 AD when Emperor Domitian ordered the uprooting of vine stocks in Provence and their replacement with grain. Rome at this time was experiencing problems and needed grain more than wine, as her soil was suitable for the vine but too poor for cereal crops. The

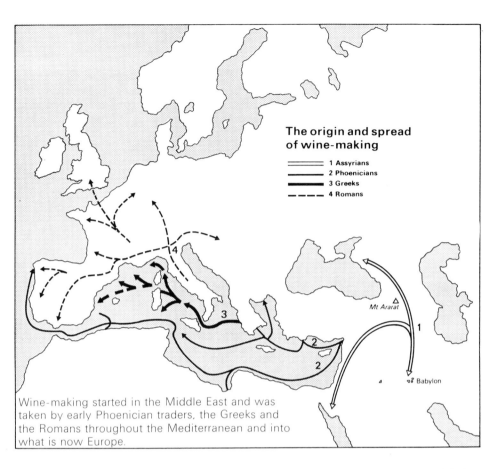

The origin and spread of wine-making

═══════ 1 Assyrians
━━━━━ 2 Phoenicians
▬▬▬▬▬ 3 Greeks
– – – – 4 Romans

Wine-making started in the Middle East and was taken by early Phoenician traders, the Greeks and the Romans throughout the Mediterranean and into what is now Europe.

wine-producing areas inland fortunately were left untouched. Many growers also disregarded the directive which was later, in 280 AD, repealed by Emperor Prubus.

Meanwhile the Roman Legions had extended their prosperity and knowledge of viticulture to the Rhône Valley, Burgundy, the Loire, Saône, Marne and Seine and later to Bordeaux.

Christianity and the vine

Unlike Islam, Christianity did not outlaw wine, so when the Roman Empire was overrun during the fifth century by Barbarians from the East, it was the early Christian missionaries with their viticultural knowledge who saved the vine. Wine was needed by the Christians for sacramental purposes so wherever they built their churches the vine flourished. Emperor Charlemagne gave his support to the church and to viticulture, and owned a vineyard at Corton, famous to this day as the great Corton Charlemagne.

Throughout the Dark Ages, it was only the religious orders, with their knowledge and dedication, who made really great wines. During the fifth century the vineyards round the great monastery of Cluny were cultivated by the monks. The Abbey of Cluny, today still impressive though in

7

ruins, was later to become one of the most powerful arms of the church in the whole of France, forever linking the history of its church with the history of wine.

Several centuries later members of the same order moved to northern Burgundy where they were bequeathed some poor uncultivated lands in the valley of the River Vouge. From that humble beginning, and with the generosity of local owners who gave them small vineyard areas, they built Clos de Vougeot, one of the finest monasteries in France. By 1336, they had completely enclosed the vineyards with a magnificent wall (clos) which still stands today—a monument to the Monks who built it.

The English connection

Bordeaux and England became irrevocably linked when, in 1152, Eleanor, daughter of

▼ The 12th-century Abbey of Clos de Vougeot, now a wine museum and a meeting place of the Confrérie des Chevaliers du Tastevin.

the last Duke of Aquitaine, married Henry Plantagenet, Count of Anjou. Henry was crowned Henry II of England just two years later. As a result of this alliance, prosperity came to Bordeaux and for 300 years their merchants sold claret to the English aristocracy.

It was during this period that the Vintners' Company, one of the 12 great livery companies of the City of London was founded. By its first charter in 1364, it was granted a monopoly control of the trade with Gascony. Consequently, the people of Bordeaux became prosperous, and elegant houses and public establishments appeared. Far sighted planners developed their city to become one of the finest in Europe with building masterpieces such as the Grand Theatre (by Victor Louis), the huge Place des Quinconces and the Place de la Bourse. The Quai des Chartrons, perhaps today a little time worn, but still stately and providing premises for members of the Bordeaux wine trade, was also built.

Such was the prosperity of Bordeaux, that even during the disastrous Hundred

▲ This section of the Bayeux Tapestry shows that wines formed an important part of the victuals for the Norman Fleet that invaded England in 1066.

Years' War (1337–1453), the Bordelais were still most conscious of their English citizenship. The end of the Middle Ages and the finish of the Hundred Years' War came at the Battle of Castillon, in 1453, when John Talbot was defeated and Bordeaux returned to France. Trade with England suffered considerably, but there was still a great demand for Bordeaux wines in London. King Louis XI of France was also conscious of the importance of the wine trade to Bordeaux and resulting from his help and support, prosperity continued.

Unlike the Bordeaux vineyards of today, those of the 17th century were small and worked mainly by tenant farmers. The draining of the marshes in the Médoc and the planting out of large areas was really the beginning of the large present day estates.

In 1797, wine from Château Lafite became the first claret to be laid down for ageing, a bottle of which is still proudly displayed at the château.

Area under direct rule of Henry II.

Area under indirect rule of Henry II or owing suzerainty to him.

Area under direct rule of King of France.

Area under indirect rule of King of France.

▲ Henry Plantagenet, Duke of Anjou, married Eleanor of Aquitaine, thus uniting this vast portion of France under the English crown on his accession to the throne.

▲ The French Revolution had important repercussions on wine production in France as large vineyards owned by the Church were parcelled out among the peasantry.

Break up of the vineyards

Whereas in Bordeaux the big vineyards were generally unaffected by the French Revolution, this was the reverse in Burgundy. Most of the larger properties belonged to the Church and these were taken from them and sold to the people, so setting up the present day system of small ownership.

The great vineyards of course still exist. But because individual growers use varying methods, the resulting wines may often have completely different characteristics even though they have the same name and were produced in the same year. An example is Clos de Vougeot, one of the largest of the Burgundian grand-cru vineyards, once owned by the Abbot of Cîteaux. It covers 50 hectares and has over 80 owners, ranging from small growers to big shipping houses. Today it is of the greatest prestige to own even the smallest portion of the vineyard.

Developing a reputation

During the 19th century, France was prosperous and considerable wealth was invested in her great vineyards, producing wines of superlative quality. In the 50 years leading up to 1870, there were more and finer wines made in these famous vineyards than had ever before been made in any of the wine-producing areas of the world.

The second half of the 19th century also brought problems for the vigneron in the form of mildew (oidium) followed by phylloxera, which nearly succeeded in devastating the vineyards of Europe (see page 27).

In recent years excise duty is probably the greatest problem the wine trade has had to face. However, the consumption of French wines continues to increase, although unfortunately the demand for certain fine wines still exceeds the supply.

The French-wine trade

While little appears to have changed in wine production over many centuries, the industry has expanded greatly since parts of the world have become more affluent and the demand for wine has increased considerably.

Today the wine industry ranges from the small grower at one end to the large national company with international connections at the other. Add to this supporting industries such as bottle manufacturers, case makers, capsule and label manufacturers and cork producers, and you have an industry that contributes greatly to the wealth of a large producing country like France.

Each facet of the industry may be covered by small or large producers. Some concentrate on perhaps just growing grapes or making wine, and then selling through brokers to marketing organizations of the larger companies and groups. Some of these groups span the whole range through production to marketing, often owning all sections of the chain from vineyard to retail outlets.

The small grower

The small grower really dominates the production of grapes, as it is he, rather than the large land owner, who produces the greatest overall quantity. Many of these people tend to limit their operation to growing and then selling their grapes to larger companies or cooperatives. Wine-producing equipment is expensive and is virtually used only for three or four weeks each year. Consequently, given the small size of many vineyards, it is uneconomic to invest in such machinery.

Cooperatives

One way round this problem is for the small farmers to band together to form cooperatives. This has occurred in many regions that have increased their production in recent years. The cooperative sets up a wine-making plant with a marketing department. The small grower simply hands over his grapes and in return receives a credit according to their quality and quantity. His share of the profit is subsequently taken when the wine is sold.

The traditional trade

The more traditional trade works through the grower, courtier, négociant chain.

▼ Because of the quantities sold, wine is often delivered by tanker to wine shops in Paris.

THE WINE TRADE

▼ Constant care of the growing vine is a necessary part of the vigneron's fight against disease and insect pests.

▼ The wine-maker needs to watch the progress of the fermenting grape juice in order to turn it into a quality wine.

▲ The courtier is a wine-broker. Because of his specialized knowledge of the vineyards in the area where he operates, he is used by a négociant or wine shipper to select and purchase wines for him.

▲ The blender applies his skill to maintain a standard product for the branded-wine market.

▼ The cooperative system enables the small grower the opportunity to make good wine without the expense of installing wine-making equipment. The cooperative will take his grapes, make them into wine and market the produce.

▼ Many of the finest vineyards were established by the wealthy, aristocratic families on the estates surrounding their elegant homes. Wines produced from these estates have become legendary in the fine-wine market.

▲ Casks usually made of oak are still widely used for storage and transport.

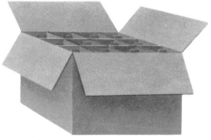

▲ Once bottled, dressed and packed in cartons, the wines are ready for sale.

▲ The road tanker is a modern economical method of transporting wine in bulk.

▲ Sea transport is used for the longer journeys, carrying wines in cartons, casks or containers.

Many vineyard owners, especially those privileged enough to own a vineyard in one of the regions maintaining a high reputation for quality, prefer to make their own wines. Such high-reputation vineyards are always in great demand, which of course means that they can charge higher prices. In turn, this helps to keep their quality consistent. Growers in this quality bracket naturally prefer to sell their wines through the courtier to the négociant.

The courtier

The courtier is a wine-broker with a great degree of expertise and knowledge of the individual vineyards. It is he who acts as the middle man between the grower and the négociant supplying the type and quality of wine required.

The négociant and agencies

The négociant is really a market house for wine, and collects large stocks to meet the needs of his market. Besides dealing in quality wines from individual vineyards and areas, the négociant will also sell his house brands, which are known as monopole wines. All his wines are supported by his reputation, and it is from them that the great names in the wine trade have appeared.

In order to extend their sales, the négociants maintain agencies in their overseas markets, such as Britain and the USA. It is mostly the established wine merchants who sell the wines supplied by them.

▼ An aerial view of Château Margaux, Premier Grand Cru 1855, showing the vineyards in the background from which have come the many great vintages of this fabulous claret.

Marketing

The wine shippers, whether small family firms or large groups, will maintain a sales force and marketing organization to promote and sell their products to restaurants, clubs, shops and supermarkets. Extensive press and television advertising is also used to draw the public's attention to particular wines. And comprehensive tastings are periodically set up to launch new products and introduce buyers to the new vintages as they become available.

Many of the larger brewery groups have the added advantage of controlling many retail outlets within their organization. And supermarkets and hypermarkets are fast competing with the traditional wine shop for a share in the market.

Restaurants

Wine is a natural accompaniment for food so restaurants play an important role in the consumption of wine. In France, where food is so close to the heart, many restaurants

▲ In contrast to the great châteaux, many cooperatives like this one at Rivesaltes in Roussillon make and market wine for the small grower.

are judged not only on their menus but also on their wine lists. The Michelin guide for Europe and the Egon Ronay guide for Britain comment meticulously on the availability, range and value for money of the wines offered in listed restaurants as well as on the excellence of the cuisine.

The end of the chain

It is of course with food that wine is finally consumed and it is here that the chain ends. Having progressed from grower to retailer, wine has covered its life cycle from grape to glass. Whether as an aperitif before a meal, an accompaniment in the home, a vin ordinaire with a hunk of cheese, one of a range of wines during a palatial banquet, a dessert at the end of a meal or merely as a draught to quench a thirsty throat, wine should always give satisfaction.

Classification of French wines

The various wines produced in France fall into certain quality categories. The factors that determine these qualities are: the area of production, the type of grape varieties, minimum alcoholic content permitted and the methods of cultivation and vinification. Some wine does not have any quality status at all and in France it is known as vin ordinaire while the British affectionately call it 'plonk'.

Vin de pays

These everyday table wines, drunk in France with ordinary meals, are simply vin ordinaire that qualifies for a very loose county status, e.g. Vin de Pays du Gard and Vin de Pays L'Hérault. Both of these are very large departments (counties) in France and the wine is ordinary but with the special privilege of using a department name. There are 33 defined areas in France producing this type of wine.

VDQS

The next status is VDQS, or to give it its full name Vins Délimités de Qualité Supérieure. This is a wine of true quality status which of course has to conform to the government rules laid down for this class of wine as to zone, grape variety and tasting tests, etc.

AC wines

The premier aristocrat, better than VDQS, is the AC or Appellation d'Origine Contrôlée wine. This category is applied only to the superior wines and represents some 17 per cent of France's total wine production. The term Appellation Contrôlée de-

notes that the wine comes from a particular area or origin which is strictly controlled for quality. It must be made from approved grape varieties in a special way according to the dictates of the region. Often the colour of the wine is specified, i.e. red only, white only or in certain circumstances red, white and rosé, and the minimum and sometimes maximum strengths of the wine are also laid down. Even the amount of wine allowed to be produced is fixed and expressed in hectolitres per hectare.

These regulations are controlled by a committee set up in 1935 under the Institut National des Appellations d'Origine des Vins et Eaux-de-Vie (the National Institute of Place names of Wines and Spirits). As a government body, the INAO were empowered to grant, in conjunction with local authorities of the area, the qualification of Appellation Contrôlée (AC) to vineyards whose wines met specified standards. If this was not enough, in many areas of rather special regions, such as Bordeaux and Burgundy, there are lists of classifications of the finest wines from single vineyards within these Appellation Contrôlée areas.

1855 classification of wines in Bordeaux

Over the years, many attempts had been made to classify the wines of Bordeaux. However, it was not until 1855 that an official classification was made for the Paris Exhibition. The Syndicat des Courtiers de Bordeaux set up a committee of Bordeaux brokers of considerable experience and integrity to classify the châteaux of the Médoc and later Sauternes. The

MAJOR CLASSIFICATIONS OF FRENCH WINES

Specific classifications
<u>Bordeaux</u>:
  1855 classification of the Médoc
  1855 classification of Sauternes and Barsac
  1955 classification of St Emilion
  1959 classification of Graves

<u>Burgundy</u>: Têtes de Cuvée

<u>Champagne</u>: Individual vineyard assessment

General classifications
Appellation Contrôlée: classification administered
  by the Institut National des Appellations
  d'Origine des Vins et Eaux-de-Vie established
  1935.

Vins Délimités de Qualité Supérieure

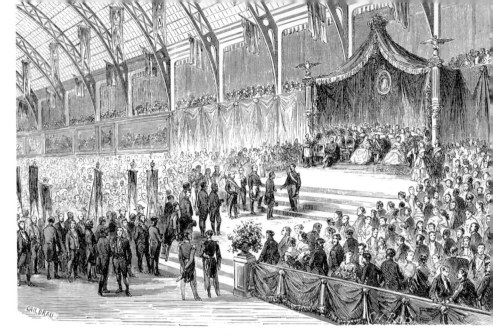

classification was based on prices paid by Bordeaux merchants over the previous century, and the wines from 62 of the best claret vineyards were selected and arranged into five grades: 4 were listed as first growths (premiers crus), 15 as second growths (deuxièmes crus), 14 as third growths (troisièmes crus), 11 as fourth growths (quatrièmes crus) and 18 as fifth growths (cinquièmes crus).

It is unfortunate that 'growths' are so often misunderstood—a third growth being assumed as a third class wine. This, of course, is not so. In fact to be included at all is outstanding, being one of 62 carefully selected from a total of over 2,000 vineyards of one of finest red-wine-producing areas in the world.

The 1855 classification is truly remarkable in that, despite changes of ownership of the vineyards, it has remained unchanged, with one exception, as a leading public guide for over 120 years. The exception was in 1973, when Château Mouton Rothschild was raised from first place in

▲ The classifications of the great wines of the Médoc and Sauternes were produced for the Great Exhibition held in Paris in 1855.

the second growth, to join the four premiers crus. There are, of course, many fine wines that over the years have greatly improved whose owners feel they are long overdue for higher grading.

1855 classification of the vineyards of Sauternes and Barsac

A similar classification was also carried out for Sauternes as was for the Médoc. But a problem arose in that one wine was so outstanding among the sweet wines of Sauternes, that it was necessary to establish a special section for it. This was Château d'Yquem, now graded as a first great growth (premier grand cru), a grading which remains unchallenged to this day.

18

ducing only white wines and a third for vineyards producing red only. Château Haut Brion, which produces both red and white wines, is listed in both the Médoc (1855) and Graves (1959) classifications.

Burgundy

Unlike Bordeaux, Burgundy has a significantly different approach to the laws of Appellation Contrôlée. In the first place, full appellations of origin are conferred on single vineyards in Burgundy whereas in Bordeaux full AC goes no lower than the commune (parish) or a collection of vineyards.

Nevertheless, in Burgundy there are various lists of the finer wines usually referred to as the Tête de Cuvée. Examples include wines such as Les Charmes in the commune of Meursault or Le Corton in the area of Aloxe.

Following d'Yquem came 11 châteaux classified as first growths and a further 12 châteaux making up the second growth. Again, as in the Médoc, they are all superb wines of their type.

1955 classification of St Emilion

Exactly one hundred years later it was the turn of the district of St Emilion to be classified. Unlike previous classifications, it was decided that two grades only would be set up. Consequently there are 12 châteaux listed as first great growths and 70 as first growths.

1959 classification of Graves

When Graves was originally classified in 1953 problems arose resulting in a revision in 1959. Even then it was not altogether satisfactory and further changes were made. Finally three classifications were set up: one for vineyards producing red and white wines, a second for vineyards pro-

The Loire

Comparatively few of the wines of the Loire are marketed under the name of the vigneron or his châteaux. Most are sold under the Appellation Contrôlée of the village or district.

Alsace

In 1962, Alsace was awarded its AOC (Appellation d'Origine Contrôlée) as a result of work by a committee of experts that had sat for 17 years. A year later, the Comité Interprofessionel du Vin d'Alsace was founded to give technical assistance to growers and to act as a liason body between growers and shippers.

Factors affecting quality

Climate

It is the fine balance between temperature, the number of hours of sunshine, rainfall and humidity that has an important bearing on the quality of wine. During the summer when the grapes are beginning to ripen, moderate rainfall and reasonably high temperatures that will not scorch the grapes are preferred.

In France, the climate varies considerably from north to south. While the ameliorating influences of the Mediterranean give hot summers and mild winters virtually free from frost in the Midi, the vigneron in Alsace and Champagne has to contend with more extreme conditions that fluctuate from year to year.

The possibility of a late spring frost spells potential disaster and consequently aspect attains considerable importance. Most vineyards are therefore planted on south-facing slopes where they maximize the number of sunshine hours and are protected from cold northerly winds. Smoke pots too are used to keep the temperature above freezing when there is threat of a frost.

Hailstorms can also cause considerable localized damage.

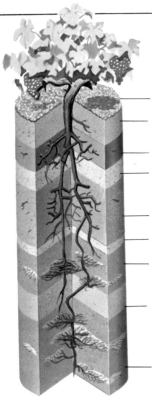

HOW A VINE GROWS

Pebbles and marl

Pebbles and sand— few roots

Marl—roots

Compacted sand

Gravel and sand with some organic matter— root system developed

Compacted sand

Rusty sand with patches of grey sand where water collects—roots infiltrate these pockets

Yellow sand

Rusty sand with patches of grey sand where water collects—roots infiltrate these pockets

Paris•

Alsace

Prevailing west wi

Soil types

Vines can be grown on a considerable range of soils each of which affects the overall characteristics of the wine. Good drainage provided by the soil structure and a slope is essential to prevent waterlogging. The subsoil should also contain sufficient nutrients on which the root system can draw.

Médoc

Sand and gravel
Clay, gravel and
some limestone

Champagne

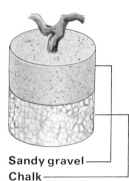

Sandy gravel
Chalk

Châteauneuf-du-Pape

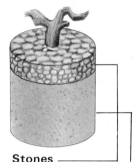

Stones
Shingles and
sandy clay

ALSACE—an anatomy of a wine-producing area

Latitude: 49°N

Types of grape: Sylvaner, Riesling
Gewürztraminer,
Muscat and Tokay d'Alsace

Climate: semi-continental
as sheltered from
prevailing winds

Low rainfall—500mm a year

Plain of Alsace

Vineyards

Most rainfall

River Rhine

Vosges Mountains
(900m)

360m

180m

The quality of wine is determined by four factors—soil, climate, vine type and the expertise of the grower.

Soil

In general the soil most suitable for making good wines could never be looked upon as good farming ground, often it is arid and stony. Bordeaux, Champagne and the Rhône valley all have poor soils yet produce world-famous wines, while the rich fertile vineyards of south-west France produce enormous quantities of wine but only vin ordinaire.

Vines produce their best fruit on well-drained soil particularly if it contains quartz, lime or slate. As the roots are forced to penetrate downwards in their search for water, they absorb 'trace (flavouring) elements' from the various layers. These elements include cobalt, copper, nickel, iodine, zinc and manganese and although

▼ Spraying the vines is an important measure in the continual fight against mildew, oidium and insect pests.

minute in quantity affect the characteristics of the vine.

The effects that various soils can have is clearly illustrated by the diverse types of wine produced from the same grape variety grown in different areas such as Champagne and Burgundy. The quality of wine can even vary in adjoining vineyards.

Climate

Climatic conditions are of course controlled by nature and, unlike soil, can only be accepted but not selected. What therefore can the vigneron hope for?—a fairly cold rainy winter, followed by a warm spring, when the buds are being formed, and a long hot summer, with moderate rainfall, and sultry humid nights. This of course is the vigneron's dream, which promises swelling buds and ripening fruit

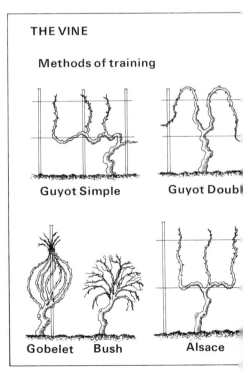

THE VINE

Methods of training

Guyot Simple   Guyot Doubl

Gobelet   Bush   Alsace

that will give him adequate sugar that can be converted into an alcoholic wine for a good vintage.

Life, however, is not without such hazards as late frosts in early May which can absolutely ruin a developing crop while hail and freak storms are the constant nightmare of the grower. Too much rain or too little sun will only produce under-ripe fruit resulting in an acid-tasting wine with low alcohol.

The vine

The large fleshy table grapes we all know so well do not usually produce good wine. The most suitable grapes are normally small and juicy, and grown in Europe from the species *Vitis vinifera*. As the finest of grapes have a relatively small yield, so it is important to grow them in the most suit-

able soil and in accordance with the local appellation laws which control density of planting and maximum yield, etc.

Expertise of the grower

Ultimately, it is the knowledge, skill and endeavour of the vigneron which produces the wine we enjoy drinking. Building on what nature provides, his expertise at pruning and protecting the vine against pests and disease helps to ensure a successful harvest.

Pruning

Pruning is so all-important to the production of quality wine that too much emphasis cannot be given to it.

This centuries-old viticultural art takes place in both winter and summer, but for different reasons. Basically, pruning is necessary to obtain a constant yield of

▼ Frost can devastate flowering vines. In Champagne smoke pots are used to raise the air temperature during such times.

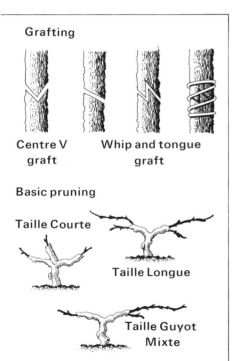

Grafting

Centre V graft   Whip and tongue graft

Basic pruning

Taille Courte

Taille Longue

Taille Guyot Mixte

grapes of a high quality each year. Failure to prune could, over a reasonably short period, cause a deterioration of the vine to an extent that neither quality nor quantity could be maintained. Winter pruning normally takes place after the harvest from December to early April, when the sap has withdrawn from the vine and before the next season's growth cycle begins. To achieve the correct balance between vine growth and the amount of crop, ruthless pruning of the previous year's wood is essential, leaving only selected buds for the new season's growth. The amount and style of pruning differs according to soil, climate, local tradition and Appellation Contrôlée regulations.

Summer pruning, which continues throughout the summer period, is a tidying operation to clean off excess shoots, to even up the foliage of the vine allowing the sun to ripen the grapes and to remove any diseased fruit.

Training

Vines are often pruned so that they grow into shapes that particular vineyards or areas have found helps the plant to produce its best fruit. It is an on-going operation over the years, with growers pruning their vines to a variety of systems:

Guyot The most popular method for producing fine wines, consists of a single trunk with one (simple) or two (double) fruiting arms. It is used in northern Europe extensively and throughout the world.

Gobelet This is a bush system used in Beaujolais in which the shoots are tied together at the top in the form of a goblet.

Lenz Moser This method is used mostly where mechanical cultivation is desirable. The rows are planted wider apart to allow the free movement of tractors and mechanical pickers, but to maintain the same growth the vines are planted closer together.

Grafting

Grafting is used to produce new strains of vine. Usually European scions are bound onto American rootstocks and there are several methods of doing this. But that most favoured by the French is the 'whip and tongue'. The grafts are then packed in boxes and covered with soil and charcoal for about three months to marry together before being planted out in nurseries. They will then be ready for planting in the vineyards the following spring.

THE GRAPE

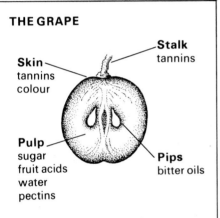

Stalk
tannins

Skin
tannins
colour

Pulp
sugar
fruit acids
water
pectins

Pips
bitter oils

The grape is the basic ingredient of all wine. Only the pips and the stalk are discarded. The skin forms a protective covering and when pressed adds tannin and colouring matter to the grape must. The pulp which forms the bulk of the grape is basically water. It contains sugars, acids —essential during fermentation and for giving brilliance and freshness to the wine—minerals and pectins which influence the flavour.

Riesling

▲ Riesling is one of the most extensively used grape varieties for white wine. The fruit is small but not very juicy. Grown mainly in Alsace, it produces dry white wine of superb flavour and outstanding bouquet.

Pinot Noir

▲ The Pinot Noir grape can produce a wine of excellent bouquet and great character. It is used for red wine in the Côte d'Or and white wine in Champagne, and is also found in rosé wines in Sancerre.

Cabernet Sauvignon

▲ Used widely in Bordeaux, Cabernet Sauvignon grapes produce deep, full-bodied red wines, that are rich in tannin and improve with age. Blended with Cabernet Franc in Anjou, it produces superb, medium-dry rosé wines.

Chardonnay

▲ Chardonnay grapes produce the great quality white wines of Montrachet, Meursault, Chablis, Pouilly Fuissé and Champagne from the Côte des Blancs. The best wines come from vines grown on clay and marly soils.

Merlot

▲ Merlot, a thick-skinned, blue-black grape, is the second most important red-wine grape in Bordeaux contributing to the delicacy of many of the classified growths of the Médoc and is used extensively in St Emilion.

Gamay

▲ Gamay, a hardy grape which grows prolifically particularly in the Beaujolais granite soil, makes light, fruity wine full of charm. It is used for VDQS wines in Auvergne and St Pourçain and in Mâconnais and the Loire.

Wine-making

Viticulture

Wine-making must inevitably start with the growing of the vine which is a long and complicated process. If you visit a vineyard you will see rows and rows of rather gnarled little bushes scarcely more than shoulder high. This gives a very false impression of the vine's true potential as it is a very long-living, prolific-growing, extremely hardy plant. For commercial wine-producing purposes the vine is cut back every year to a mere bush, and on average uprooted every 40 years.

The seasonal round

The yearly cycle of work is basically the same for all wine growing regions. But it is naturally modified from area to area to suit local conditions, hence the numerous methods of pruning and training.

Winter

After the grapes have been picked and the harvest is over, very little is done in the vineyard before the winter sets in. Some general tidying up might take place, perhaps even cutting away the straggling branches. The soil between the rows is ploughed and piled up over the roots to protect them during the winter months. The vines are then left alone to recuperate for next year's growth.

Spring

In spring, when the worst of the bad weather is over, and before the sap starts rising, the vine must be pruned and trained according to local styles. This usually means that all the surplus wood, except for perhaps just two fruiting arms, is cut away and the two arms left tied down to the wires or trained in whatever method is appropriate. The soil is then ploughed away from the roots so that the spring rains will encourage growth.

Summer

In late spring, buds appear and in early summer flowering starts. About a hundred

▼ Winter often brings snow to the northern vineyards.

▼ The vines are pruned before the start of the growing season in spring.

ENEMIES OF THE VINE

There are a number of insects that can attack and damage either the leaves and flowers or the roots of the vine but of all of them the tiny insect *Phylloxera vastatrix* has been the most disastrous adversary. This small bug found its way over the Atlantic from America in about the middle of the 19th century and by the 1890s had caused such havoc in the vineyards that many people feared wine production would come to an end. Phylloxera attacked the vine both above and below the ground, but it was the root damage that was most severe.

Fortunately, it was discovered that the American species of the vines *Vitis riparia* and *Vitis berlandieri* were immune to the ravages of this insect. But these vines produced poor grapes, making wine with a foxy unpalatable flavour, and so were not a very satisfactory substitute. However, by growing the American vine and then

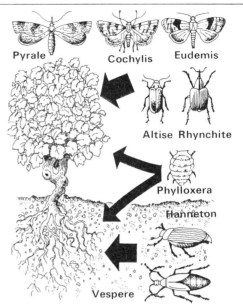

cutting it right down to root level and grafting onto it the more desirable European *Vitis vinifera* species, the effects of the insect attack were overcome.

days after this, the fruit will be ripe enough to pick. During flowering, it is vital that there are no late frosts which could kill the flowers and so stop the fruit from appearing. Understandably, the vigneron has many anxious, sleepless nights and will rush out to his vineyards to light smoke-pots or bonfires, or even to spray his vines with water, in order to keep the dreaded frosts at bay.

▼ Nets are sometimes used in summer to protect the ripe grapes from birds.

▼ Autumn brings the pickers into the vineyards for the grape harvest.

THE WINE-MAKING PROCESS

The techniques used to make wine vary from region to region and the skills handed down from generation to generation. However, the basic processes remain the same. The only difference in producing red and white wines is that for red wines the skins of red grapes are fermented with the juice and it is this which gives the red colour of varying hues.

The red grapes are usually de-stalked and the skins cracked before going into the fermenting vessel.

Red or white grapes to be made into white wine are put into a press and the juice only run off into the fermenting vessel. For rosé wines the skins are allowed to remain with the juice for only as long as is needed to produce the required pink colour.

In these fermenting

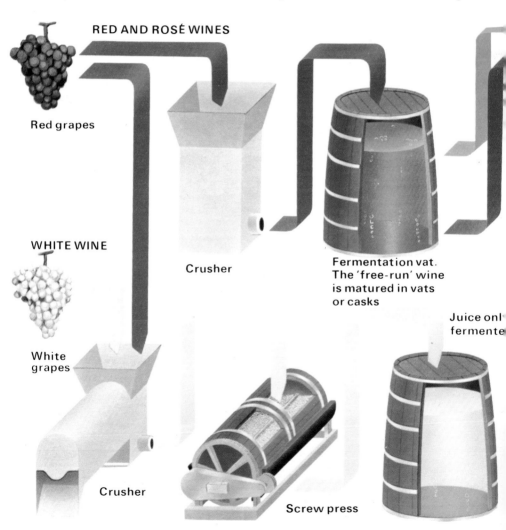

RED AND ROSÉ WINES

Red grapes

WHITE WINE

White grapes

Crusher

Crusher

Screw press

Fermentation vat. The 'free-run' wine is matured in vats or casks

Juice only fermented

vessels the enzymes in the yeast work on the grape sugar producing about ten per cent of alcohol and transforming the grape juice into wine. When fermentation is complete the wine is run off into casks or vats for a period of maturation. For fine wines, such as claret and Burgundy, this can be for as long as two to three years before being bottled.

If a sparkling wine is being made, further yeast and sugar is added to the wine before bottling which after clarification will become bright and effervescent. When mature, the wine will be bottled, corked, capsuled and labelled, ready for the consumer on the home or export market. EEC labelling regulations demand that specific details, showing the wines quality and designation must appear on the labels, so making selection much easier for the purchaser.

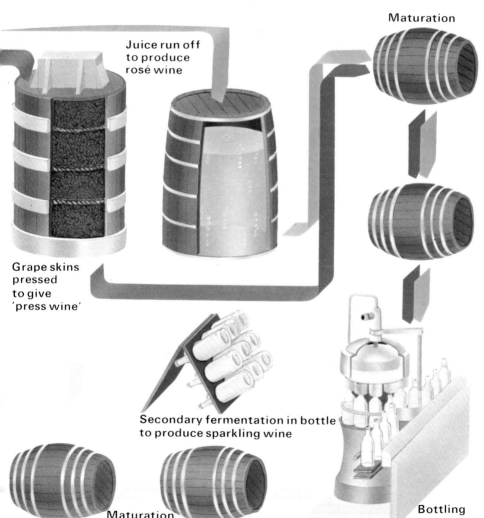

Maturation

Juice run off to produce rosé wine

Grape skins pressed to give 'press wine'

Secondary fermentation in bottle to produce sparkling wine

Maturation

Bottling

▲ Wine presses vary from region to region. These in Champagne hold four tonnes of grapes at each pressing.

grapes being picked by workers in a festive mood.

Once the grapes have formed, a whole new set of problems appear to keep him busy. Diseases such as mildew and oidium, and insect pests such as the cochylis and eudemis moths appear. So the vines have to be sprayed to protect them from damage.

Towards the end of the summer, work in the vineyard stops and during August and early September the vigneron can do little more than pray for the weather to be hot, sunny and dry until his precious harvest has been gathered in.

Harvesting

The harvest, or vendange, takes place mainly during September, a little earlier perhaps in the south of France and a little later in the northern vineyards. It is essential that the weather is dry in the period before the harvest and during the picking, and is also free of hail storms that could bruise the grapes and cause them to rot before they can be gathered in. The vintage is usually a time of great joy and celebration in the vineyard areas with the

Vinification

The wine grower completes his job by delivering luscious, ripe grapes to the press house, where the quite simple process of turning the juice (must) into wine is carried out. However, while there is a broad over-all technique for the fermentation of the grape, methods do differ slightly as, for example, in the making of white Alsatian and red Bordeaux wines.

Red, White and Rosé

Both red (sometimes called black) and white grapes produce a white juice. It is the pigment in the skin that can only give the wine colour. In order to produce red wine, red grapes are pressed but are only de-stalked and cracked in a machine called a *fouloir egrappoir* just before the juice is run into the fermenting vessel. The skins therefore have time to impart the characteristic red colouring in the wine.

In contrast, white wines may be made from either red or white skinned grapes.

▲ Fermenting vessels vary considerably from small casks to extremely large, stainless-steel vats.

▲ The finished wine needs time to mature in cellars such as these at Chinon in the Loire.

The grapes are crushed and the skins, pips and stalks immediately discarded while the juice is quickly run off for fermentation.

To make sparkling wine, still dry table wine must first be made to which a measured amount of sugar solution and cultured yeast is added. The wine then undergoes a secondary fermentation in either bottle or tank producing carbon dioxide gas which is dissolved in the wine. It is this which gives rise to the sparkle when the bottle is opened.

The pale pink colour of rosé wine is not made by blending red and white wine together. Instead, red grapes are fermented with their skins for a very short period (12 to 36 hours) before the juice is run off to continue fermenting without the skins to deepen the colour.

Fermentation

Fermentation is the essential process which turns ordinary grape juice into wine by enabling alcohol and carbon dioxide to be produced in the must. This results from a complex series of chemical reactions basically between the sugars in the juice and enzymes (proteins) carried in yeast cells.

On the skin of every grape, there are millions of wild yeasts, thousands of wine yeasts and numerous moulds and bacteria of which only the acetobacter is of any significance to the wine maker. In its simplest form, uncontrolled or natural fermentation has three clear stages. First the more numerous, but less hardy, wild yeasts attack the grape juice and convert some of the sugar into about four per cent of alcohol by volume. This is an insufficient amount for wine and at the same time the wild yeasts leave an off taste that will taint the end product. The wine yeasts then take over and carry on building up the alcoholic content to something like ten per cent, or a little more in exceptional circumstances. This is an adequate level for wine but if nature were to continue her course the vinegar bacteria would now come into action and convert the wine into vinegar.

Controlled fermentation

From the wine producer's point of view natural fermentation poses two major problems, namely the wild yeasts producing only four per cent of alcohol and an unpalatable taste, and the effects of the vinegar bacteria. Consequently it is important to eliminate these unwanted elements. This can be done by adding an oxygen inhibitor, usually sulphur dioxide, to the must as both the aerobic wild yeasts and acetobacter require oxygen. This allows the anaerobic wine yeasts, not needing oxygen, to survive and therefore carry out the whole function of fermentation, leaving a clear wine of adequate strength.

Other controlling factors

Yeast can only survive between about 4 and 33°C, and tends to work faster when hot and slower when cold. This gives the wine maker yet another means of controlling the nature of the wine. He can carry out either a cool, slow fermentation or a short, hot one. Local temperatures will also contribute to this, as it can be very hot in the south and quite cool in the north when the grapes are being picked.

The amount of sugar in the wine can also be varied. The best known method is to leave picking the grapes until well after the normal vintage, allowing them to become over-ripe and shrivelled, and thus increasing the sugar and reducing the water content. This method, known as *Pourriture Noble*, Noble Rot, is used expertly in the making of great Sauternes wines from Bordeaux. Another method is to stop the fermentation before it is completed, so retaining the original grape sugar and at the same time increasing the alcohol content—a method used in the vin doux naturel wines such as Muscat de Beaumes-de-Venise or Frontignan.

The final stages

When fermentation is complete, which takes 10 to 12 days according to the district, the must is run off into barrels. Here a secondary fermentation sets up, so the bung of each barrel is fitted with a glass breather cap to allow the gasses to escape.

When the secondary fermentation has ceased, time is allowed for the wine to become subdued and for the sediment to settle at the bottom of the barrel. It is then racked off into another barrel, and this operation is repeated until the wine is bright and clear. Very fine wines can be aged in wood for over three years and are then bottled.

A newly bottled wine is not yet ready for consumption. Even the light red wines should be aged for a year or more before being served and most of the great red wines require a much longer time.

▼ Modern bottling lines can fill, cork, capsule and label wine in one continuous operation.

The major wine-producing areas

The major-wine producing regions of France are fairly evenly distributed throughout the country and cover about 1·25 million hectares. However, the quality and quantity of wine produced varies from area to area. Languedoc-Roussillon in the Midi, for example, contributes around 40 per cent of the overall output but produces very little quality wine, while Bordeaux and Burgundy, contributing about ten and four per cent respectively produce many outstanding vintages that are eagerly sought on the world market.

Bordeaux

Bordeaux and wine have been inextricably linked for many centuries. The wines are produced in the Gironde department which before 1790 was part of the old province of Guyenne. It is the largest department in France with about a quarter of its land area devoted to vines. On average, it produces around four million hectolitres of wine annually, or as much as ten per cent of the country's total, of which some 90 per cent are AC or quality wines.

The city and port of Bordeaux lie on the Garonne River, near to where it joins with the Dordogne to form the Gironde Estuary. Although basically a sea port, it is one of the largest cities in France and capital of the Gironde department.

The Bordeaux district, or Bordelais, produces both red and white wines. The many varieties and types of reds have for centuries been known as claret. The department consists of six principal districts carefully mapped out with official boundaries. In these districts are smaller areas called communes in which are vineyards and individual châteaux. Unlike the great properties of the Loire, these are often no bigger than large country houses.

The roads are hedgeless and often dusty with occasional fir trees and straggling villages. In addition to the great estates in Bordeaux, there are many small farmer-growers who sell their produce to the big shippers or to the cooperatives mostly for blending.

The diversity of the wines is matched by an equal diversity of soils. The vines themselves over the centuries have been so selected and developed that today's estate owners know which type of vine is most suited to their own particular soil. The soils on which the vines are grown are rarely suitable for other crops, being mostly stony and sandy gravel of varying depths with a limestone or clay mixed subsoil.

The climate is tempered by the Atlantic gulf stream, with warm, and even hot, summers with a fair amount of rain in winter. A problem in the area is the danger of frost sometimes as late as May.

Médoc

North of the city on a long spit of land dividing the Gironde from the Atlantic, is

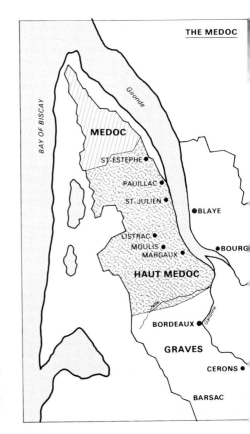

► The owners of Château Mouton Rothschild commission a new bottle label for each vintage. This one is particularly interesting in that it was designed by Picasso shortly before he died.

PABLO PICASSO BACCHANALE MUSÉE DE MOUTON

the Médoc. The area is rarely more than 15 kilometres wide and extends north for nearly 100 kilometres to where the estuary enters the sea. It is sub-divided into the communes (parishes) of St Estèphe, Margaux, St Julien and Pauillac. Within these parishes are the famous estates that give their names to the great clarets. The well-drained, gravelly soil is particularly suited to the production of fine red wine. And it is a well-known saying that the best wines come from vines grown on such soil overlooking the river. The vineyards round St Estèphe and Pauillac are extremely dense, but elsewhere they alternate with woodlands and other cultivation.

Under appellation laws, the principal grapes produced in the Médoc are the Cabernet Sauvignon, Cabernet Franc, Merlot, Malbec and Petit Verdot. No other grapes are allowed. The great red wines are outstanding for their finesse and bouquet, with body that varies with the soil throughout the area. The style of wines in individual and neighbouring communes can vary considerably. For example, in the commune of Pauillac, Château Lafite is more delicate than the fuller flavoured Château Mouton Rothschild. Broadly, Pauillac and St Estèphe produce the biggest wines, with Margaux the most delicate and St Julien taking a middle course in between.

Many of the classed growths have become very expensive. There are, however, numerous châteaux producing lesser excellent wines in the Médoc under brand names. These are known as crus bourgeois, an outstanding example being Mouton

Cadet produced in Pauillac and claimed as being the best selling claret in the world.

Graves

Next, after the Médoc, among the wines of Bordeaux, must be placed Graves. The area comprises a 16-kilometre wide strip that runs parallel to the western bank of the Garonne and for about 50 kilometres south of Bordeaux. As the name indicates, the soil is mostly of stony, sandy gravel, with a subsoil of limestone and clay.

Graves produces both red and white wines, with white wines outnumbering red and completely dominating in the south. The superb red wines live long in bottle and are in great demand. Outstanding among their fine estates is Château Haut Brion, a premier cru in the official classification of 1855, producing one of the best red wines in Bordeaux. Other world-famous properties include Châteaux Pape-Clément, La Mission Haut-Brion, Haut-Bailly, and Carbonnieux all making superb red wine.

Wine from this district was first known in England over 500 years ago. It is recorded that in 1663 Samuel Pepys 'drank a sort of French wine called "Ho Bryen" that hath a good and most particular taste that I never met'. Château Haut Brion is believed to have existed from the early 16th century. The vineyard itself is on deep gravel giving excellent drainage which, together with the heat reflecting properties of the gravel, helps always to produce good wine even in poor years. However, it was not until the turn of the 19th century that white wine was first produced at the château. Today from three hectares, around 68 hectolitres of superb, dry white wine are made annually.

Graves red wines, though not always possessing the mellowness, finesse and delicacy of the Médocs, have body, vigour and brilliant colour giving them a distinct character of their own. As they are produced from the Cabernet Sauvignon, Cabernet Franc, Merlot and Malbec grapes, they also have a family connection with the wines of the Médoc.

The best white wines of Graves are dry, fruity and with considerable flavour. Over the last 20 years improved methods of vinification have produced more acceptable wines, cleaner and crisper with balanced acidity. The best of the dry white Graves, classified in 1959, includes such

famous vineyards as Châteaux Carbonnieux, Chevalier, Couhins, Olivier and La Tour-Martillac. These wines, produced from the Sémillon, Sauvignon and Muscadelle grapes, show character, body and finesse, and some are even compared in quality with famous Médoc reds.

In the lesser quality wines, there are two appellations, Graves and Graves Supérieures. These differ little in their indication of quality, only on alcoholic strength, the latter being the stronger.

Entre-Deux-Mers

This area, about 65 kilometres long by 15 broad, lies between the rivers Garonne and

◀ The working corner of Château d'Yquem at harvest time shows grapes being delivered into the chai for processing.

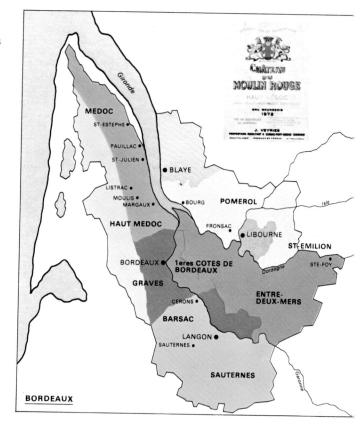

▲ Château Haut Brion, Premier Grand Cru Classé, is famous for its excellent dry white wine.

Dordogne from where it takes its name (between two seas). It is richly planted with vines and produces less distinguished, predominantly white wines. Like Graves, the red wines are found mostly in the north, but as the appellation laws only apply to the white wines, they can only be sold under the generic name of Bordeaux Rouge. There is a considerable variation of soil over the area, the better wines more suitable for export coming from the sandy clay region.

Up until the early 1960s, Entre-Deux-Mers made mostly sweet and very sweet white wines. Today much drier wines are made, a large proportion in the 15 big modern cooperatives, some of which can produce over 13,600 hectolitres annually. Most of the wine goes for blending, otherwise it is sold under the name of Entre-Deux-Mers rather than by château or parish names.

The red wines are made by a process of vatting the grapes for about five days with carbon dioxide added. The weight of the grapes breaks the skins and begins the vinification cycle. They are then taken out, pressed and re-vatted for a further six to eight days. The final result is a fresh, young wine, considerably reduced in tannin, but not outstanding in character, which will be ready for bottling in less than six months.

Viticulture is mostly by the high culture

system, which spaces the vines wider apart and much taller than usual to allow tractors to work in between the rows. This results in increased production from the same number of vines.

There are a number of sub-districts within the Entre-Deux-Mers' area which in good years make very pleasing and acceptable wines. These are dealt with in a later chapter.

Cérons

Wines from Cérons are far better known in France than elsewhere. The area is still officially part of the Graves district and is situated to the south on the Garonne River. The gravel and flint soil with a stony and clay subsoil enable a delicate white wine to be produced which in style is transitional between the dry Graves and rich Sauternes. A small amount of red wine is made but it is not outstanding.

Sauternes and Barsac

Still an area within the Graves district, Sauternes comprises five communes: Barsac, Bommes, Fargues, Preignac and Sauternes. Each was once separate but with limited production. To make them competitive in world markets, they decided to join under one appellation, that of Sauternes. As so often happens, there was one exception—Barsac—which, in view of the difference in characteristics, flavour and popularity was given its own appellation. This has given rise to a situation where Barsac is a Sauternes but not all Sauternes are Barsacs.

When producing wines in this area, the grapes are left on the vines until they are over-ripe and partly shrivelled. A micro-organism then attacks individual grapes giving them the special characteristics of sweetness and high alcoholic content which are found in fine Sauternes. This is known as Noble Rot or *Pourriture Noble*. Harvest is delayed until this has taken place and then many hours of laborious work are needed to pick sufficient grapes to make even a single hogshead of wine. Often it is necessary for a vineyard to be picked many times to collect suitably rotted grapes, this being a grape by grape operation which has been known not to finish until late November and even December.

▼ The grapes to make Sauternes are left on the vines long after the normal vintage to become over-ripe and shrivelled. This is called *Pourriture Noble* or Noble Rot.

► The old abbey ruins dominate this St-Emilion vineyard. Unlike the very flat, gravel vineyards of the Médoc, St Emilion rises gently over a subsoil of limestone.

The grapes used are mainly Sémillon and Sauvignon with about five per cent Muscadelle. The Sémillon, though not giving much in quantity, greatly adds to the quality of the wine. After de-stalking, the grapes are pressed three times and the juice run into casks to ferment and mature.

Within the five communes, certain individual vineyards are outstanding. The world-renowned Château d'Yquem is reputed to produce the finest sweet wine in the world, but very closely followed by Château Coutet, and others.

In white wine, great age is not necessarily a good quality. Sauternes, however, when from a great vintage do keep well and have been found still bright and acceptable even at 30 years and over. When too old though, they will turn brown and lose all their distinctive character.

St Emilion and Pomerol

CHATEAU AUSONE
SAINT-EMILION
APPELLATION SAINT EMILION CONTROLEE
1961
V⁰ C. VAUTHIER & J. DUBOIS CHALLON
PROPRIÉTAIRES A SAINT EMILION (GIRONDE)
MIS EN BOUTEILLES AU CHATEAU

St Emilion is one of the oldest and most picturesque wine villages in France. Situated on the eastern side of the Dordogne, it looks down from its hilltop site over more than 2,600 hectares of vineyards closely gathered on the hillside below. In addition to producing large quantities of excellent red wine, the area is steeped in history. In earlier years, it served as a resting place for pilgrims from the north on their way to Spain. Most of the town is built from local stone, the old quarries from where it was taken now making fine, wine cellars where the St Emilion wines mature.

The soil is mostly clay, stone and limestone on a subsoil of gravel—the opposite to the soil of the Médoc. Unlike elsewhere in the Bordeaux district, maturation continues in the big fermentation vats throughout the winter. In spring, tradition is again broken when the new wine is put into old casks. The wines of St Emilion are often described as the Burgundies of Bordeaux. They gain considerable delicacy after short bottle ageing, but do not, however, have the longevity of the Médoc wines.

Pomerol, the neighbouring district to the north, makes wines with much the same characteristics as St Emilion. The estates vary greatly in size and are often no bigger than small family plots. The soil is sandier and more pebbly but with a similar subsoil.

Famous vineyards in the St Emilion area include Châteaux Cheval Blanc, Ausone, Canon and Bel-air, while Pomerol has Châteaux Petrus, La Fleur and Trotanoy.

▲ The vineyard at Château Le Cone Taillasson Sabourin in the Côtes de Blaye.

Bourg and Blaye

On the east bank of the Gironde Estuary facing the Médoc country are the regions of Bourg and Blaye. They form one of the most picturesque areas of the river. Red and white wines are made in both regions, Blaye making more white than red, while in Bourg red predominates. The soil tends to be too rich and so produces mostly only average quality wines which are not very well known outside France. As in the Médoc, the best vineyards are within sight of the Gironde.

The two old towns of Bourg and Blaye are only about eight kilometres apart and are even more alike than their wines. The vineyards of Bourg make red wines similar to the bourgeois growths of the Médoc, robust and colourful, in some ways not unlike the lesser wines from St Emilion. In comparison red wines from the Blaye district are generally luscious, but rather insipid, and often used for blending. Much of the wine in these districts is sold direct to customers in France. The better wines from the estates are Côtes de Bourg and Côtes de Blaye.

The wines of Bourg and Blaye cannot be expected to compete on quality terms against the wines from across the river, although the ever increasing shortage of reasonably priced wines is causing buyers to look again at this area.

Other areas

In addition to the six main districts in the Bordeaux area there are numerous smaller districts, some well known and producing sound and acceptable wines, others lesser known and making wines of a lower grade.

Sainte Croix-du-Mont and Loupiac

Sainte Croix-du-Mont, facing Sauternes over the Garonne River, produces sweet, white wines. Though less distinguished than the great Sauternes, the wines are made from similar grape varieties, namely Sauvignon, Sémillon and a small amount of Muscadelle. Similarly, the grapes are picked late so as to allow them to be attacked by *Pourriture Noble*. Under normal conditions they are good wines but not great.

Adjoining Sainte Croix-du-Mont to the north, Loupiac is practically identical to its neighbour in every respect, so much so that they are often regarded as one.

Graves de Vayres

This is an area between Bordeaux and Libourne on the Dordogne River which produces red and white wines from a soil of sand, gravel and chalk. The red wines, though delicate and crisp, cannot compete with the best from St Emilion across the river. The white wines are mellow, delicate and crisp, and outnumber the reds by some five to one.

Fronsac

The small district of Fronsac lies to the west of Pomerol and about three kilometres north of Libourne. This medieval town has two appellations, Côte de Fronsac and Côtes Canon Fronsac. The latter is situated on the Cânon hills which overlook the Dordogne River. Both red and white wines are produced though only red qualifies for appellation grading. The countryside is picturesque and though producing good wines, due to a somewhat rich soil, they lack the quality of their St Emilion and Pomerol neighbours.

Premières Côtes de Bordeaux

The Premières Côtes de Bordeaux vineyards extend along the east bank of the Garonne on the low hills bordering the river and running south for nearly 50 kilometres. The area produces red and white wines. The whites, ranging from dry to sweet, outnumber the reds by six to one and are superior wines.

Arsac and Labarde

There are a number of lesser known communes in the Médoc producing excellent Bourgeois and Bourgeois Supérieurs wines. Arsac, for example, a small commune, has one fifth-growth vineyard, Château Le Tertre, and two Crus Bourgeois Supérieurs, Châteaux d'Arsac and Monbrison, producing mostly red wines. Labarde has one third-growth vineyard, Château Giscours, a fifth-growth, Château Dauzac, and three Crus Bourgeois Supérieurs which include Château Siran.

▼ These grapes, though perhaps not of such noble birth as their classified brethren, will produce good AC Bordeaux wine.

Burgundy

This fascinating corner of France, once the home of the powerful Dukes of Burgundy and steeped in tradition, is today the holiday-maker's dream and a gastronomic paradise for the gourmet. Midst a rich rolling countryside and vine-clad hills, superb wines are made, the best of which can stand alongside the finest in the world. Because of its position deep in central France, Burgundy has a continental climate with very hot summers and often severe winters—it is the most northern area in Europe that produces great red wine.

Burgundy stretches from Chablis in the north west through the whole length of the Côte d'Or, a low range of protecting hills rising 60 to 90 metres from the level of the plain, the Côte Chalonnaise, Mâconnais and Beaujolais to Villefranche-sur-Saône. It is a region nearly 210 kilometres in length varying in width from less than two kilometres in the Côte d'Or up to several kilometres in Beaujolais, with a break of about 65 kilometres between Chablis and Dijon.

The Côte d'Or is divided into two sections the Côte de Nuits in the north and the Côte de Beaune in the south.

The vineyards are much smaller than those of Bordeaux and there are few big estates. The vineyards, which average around half a hectare, are mostly owned and worked by peasant farmers and their families.

Red Burgundies are made from two grape varieties which differ according to the need. The Pinot Noir produces fine red wines of great character finesse and delicacy, but is difficult to grow. The red wines of the Côte d'Or are made from this but the whites come from the Chardonnay grape. Lesser wines are made from the Gamay (red) and the Aligote (white) grapes, mostly in southern Burgundy.

Passe-tous-grains is the vatting together of one third Pinot and two thirds Gamay grapes. Though producing a pleasant wine, mostly drunk locally, it does not travel well. By law it must have at least 9.5 per cent alcohol. Bourgogne Mousseux is a sparkling red or white wine, entitled to its own appellation but carrying a higher duty.

As recently as the turn of the century, red Burgundies were given much longer periods of vatting than today, when, resulting from longer periods of fermentation, they developed more tannin and thus a longer life. The demand for Burgundy and the escalation of costs, however, necessitated a reduction in vatting time.

Although the cooperative system plays an important part in Beaujolais and the Mâconnais and to a lesser degree in Chablis, in general vignerons vinify their own grapes or, as often in the Côte de Nuits, sell the grapes direct to a négociant.

The process of chaptalization, which was introduced by a Doctor Chaptal, requires the addition of sugar to the must to build up the alcoholic strength by a maximum of 2°. Under French law, this is allowed in Burgundy because of its northerly position

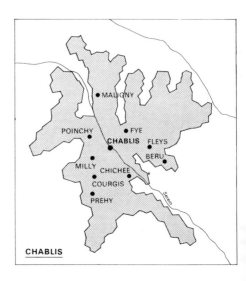

CHABLIS

▲ Chablis, the detached, most northerly part of Burgundy, produces only white wine. This premier cru vineyard will pick its grapes a little later than vineyards in the sunnier south.

which means in some years the grapes are unable to produce sufficient sugar to make a stable wine. The fermenting wine is strictly controlled by inspectors, who can authorize the addition of quantities of sugar up to a maximum of 200 kilos per hectare of vines.

Chablis

Petit Chablis
APPELLATION CONTROLÉE
PRODUIT DE FRANCE

SHIPPED AND BOTTLED BY
e   HEDGES & BUTLER LTD   35cl
LONDON W.1.

Chablis is often described as the 'Golden Gate' of Burgundy although it is situated in a somewhat isolated area. It produces very

dry, flinty, white wines that are in demand by wine merchants and hoteliers throughout the world, as they are a splendid accompaniment to fish and all types of shellfish. But because production is only around 11,370 hectolitres, availability is always a problem.

The Chardonnay vines are grown on the gently rolling hills that overlook the town. They are trained close to the ground so as to obtain the maximum amount of warmth particularly in view of the severe frosts experienced at times even as late as May. The soil is infertile and a bituminous kimmeridgian clay subsoil gives a sparse covering to the underlying rock. Where the vines are planted on steep slopes, the soil is often washed away and has to be replaced manually. Traditionally when a vineyard has been uprooted, it has been left fallow for up to 20 years. Modern chemical techniques, however, now considerably reduce this period.

There are four categories of Chablis. The first is Chablis Grands Crus which can be applied to seven special vineyards on the hills north-east of the village obtaining best advantage from the sun. The area and quantity of wine produced, however, is very small. Second, the category of Chablis Premier Cru covers wines made in 18 communes in the vicinity of Chablis. The third category, Chablis without a vineyard name, comprises wines of lesser strength and character while the last division, Petit Chablis, includes wines from the same district that do not have the same quantity of alcohol.

Growers in Chablis often own a number of separate small plots which can total from less than one hectare to more than 12. As a result shippers will blend the wines of different growers from the same vineyard area under their own shipping or company name. Other growers produce their own grapes and bottle the wine themselves.

Côte
de Nuits

The Côte de Nuits begins at Fixin, three kilometres south of Dijon, and follows the 'Route des Grands Crus', lined on either side with vineyards, ending below the principal town of Nuits. In this small area of only 30 square kilometres, some of the greatest red wines in the world are made from the Pinot grape. The soil is a reddish clay with small chalky pebbles, and rich in calcium, magnesium, lime, potassium and phosphorus. The subsoil is mostly flinty

▼ The Confrérie des Chevaliers du Tastevin, in their colourful costumes, meet to invest new members.

clay mixed with chalk. Consequently, the wines are robust with considerable bouquet and more body than the wines of the neighbouring areas.

The vineyard at Clos de Vougeot has for many years been a major tourist attraction. Apart from being a beautifully-maintained vineyard, it is the meeting place of the world-famous Burgundian Brotherhood, the Confrérie des Chevaliers du Tastevin. Today the members are mostly growers, shippers and visiting dignitaries who meet frequently to further the promotion of Burgundian wines.

Although the Côte de Nuits is always regarded as an entire red-wine-producing area, there are the odd small amounts of white wine produced, as in the communes of Chambolle-Musigny and Vougeot, both from the Chardonnay grape.

Côte
de Beaune

The vineyards of the Côte de Beaune stretch for 24 kilometres from the famous limestone quarry where the Côte de Nuits finishes to the south of Santenay. The area produces double the quantity of wine made in the Côte de Nuits from larger but less well known vineyards. Though lacking the elegance and fragrance of their famous neighbours, the wines can be characterized by their bouquet and delicacy, and by the fact that they are consistently good.

The vineyard road leads straight into the town of Beaune, the commercial centre and wine capital of the Côte d'Or, which gives its name to the vine slopes to the north and south. It is an old walled town housing vineyard owners' and shippers' cellars.

The celebrated Hospice de Beaune, a 15th century hospital for the aged, owns many excellent vineyards throughout the region and its wines are sold by auction each year on the second Sunday in November. The ceremony at the sale is picturesque, and on the day, the town is crowded with buyers who taste the new wine before making bids. The prices reached at the sale serve as a guide to the year's prices of Burgundy wines. The sale is followed by a banquet in the Hospice with similar functions over the weekend in Beaune, Clos de Vougeot, and Meursault.

The finest red wine in the Côte de Beaune comes from near the village of Aloxe with its great vineyard Le Corton acclaimed by the Dukes of Burgundy and Voltaire. Other outstanding vineyards (Têtes de Cuvée) include Les Grèves (Beaune), Les Epenots (Pommard), Santenay (Volnay), Les Bressandes (Aloxe).

In the commune of Aloxe Corton, excellent white Burgundy from Corton-Charlemagne is produced, which in great years, can be classed with the great Montrachets. The wines from this area are made from the Chardonnay grape and are big and golden.

South of Volnay, the vineyards of Meursault, produce what must be among the finest, dry, white wines in the world. Meursault is an old garrison town, reputed to date back to Roman occupation, and is today very prosperous. Its straw-coloured wines are delicate and perfumed and somewhat less dry than the flinty Chablis. Full red wine is also produced in the district but cannot be compared with the magnificent whites.

On from Meursault, through the village of Puligny, is one of the greatest white-wine vineyards in the world—Montrachet. The individual vineyards are walled, with broken stone arches leading into the numerous plots. The greatest of the great is the Montrachet itself, which in a good year

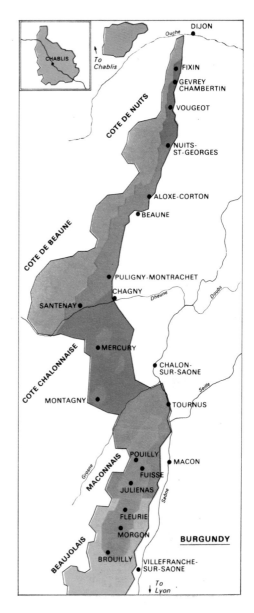

rarely produces 250 hectolitres—France alone could easily absorb a hundred times that amount. Surrounding the incomparable Montrachet are the other top ranking vineyards of Bâtard Montrachet, Le Cheva-

45

▶ The undulating hills of Beaujolais are portrayed here in this vineyard at Chénas. All but the very high ground is planted with vines.

Far right. The happy, homely, people of Beaujolais not only love their wine but are proud to tell the world so, and are seen here in festival mood at their annual wine fête.

lier-Montrachet, Puligny-Montrachet and Chassagne-Montrachet.

The white wines of Chassagne have an unmistakable flavour, dry but not hard, and a little less steely than those of Puligny. They somewhat overshadow the reds which nevertheless are soft and well balanced, falling between the lighter Burgundies of Beaujolais and those of the Côte d'Or, and excellent value.

Below Chassagne is the last town of the Côte d'Or, Santenay, which produces practically all red wines, not outstanding but sound. They are rarely sold under individual vineyard names.

fertile. And they are planted mainly with Pinot Noir, Pinot Blanc and Chardonnay vines. Apart from the communes of Givry, Mercurey, Rully and Montagny, other areas only produce red and white wines of average quality.

Chalonnais

The vineyards of Chalonnais are situated on the low hills facing the Saône River between Chagny and Tournus—an area sometimes confused as an extension of the Côte de Beaune. However, the red and white wines are of a lesser quality but in good years are most acceptable. The vineyards cover about 18,000 hectares on soil similar to that of the Côte de Beaune, though more

Mâconnais

Good, sound, red and white Mâcon wines have for centuries been eagerly sought on the world markets. The red is produced from the Gamay grape while the Chardonnay and Aligoté are used for the white. The limestone and slate soil, notably between Pouilly Fuissé and Mâcon and further north with the inclusion of chalky oolite, is particularly suited to the produc-

tion of dry, white wine. Consequently, Mâconnais is most applauded for such a wine—the magnificent Pouilly Fuissé.

Beaujolais

Beaujolais is possibly the most familiar of French wine names. It appears on nearly every wine list and is found in most retailing outlets both inside and outside France. Ruby red in colour, the wine is made from Gamay grapes that thrive on the granite soil on the gentle slopes of the rather hilly countryside. Although Beaujolais has a number of large vineyards, in general it is an area of small vignerons each on average with about four hectares of land. It is understandable, therefore, that 18 co-operative cellars account for the vinification of about 30 per cent of production.

In normal years, the area produces around 91 million litres, or nearly 70 per cent of the total red wine of Burgundy. This can be divided into three grades — Beaujolais, Beaujolais Supérieur and Beaujolais Villages—and nine classified growths— Saint Amour, Juliénas, Chénas, Moulin-à-Vent, Fleurie, Chiroubles, Morgon, Brouilly and Côte de Brouilly. A small amount of white wine is also produced from the Pinot Chardonnay grape in the northern region of Haut Beaujolais.

In recent years a lot of fun (and business) has developed in Western Europe and the USA from the desire to drink Beaujolais Nouveau, a very young wine. There is an annual race of buyers to buy the new wine on 15 November, the first permitted day for selling following the vintage, and then to transport it as quickly as possible to, for example, London. Preparation for the journey necessitates several early rackings to clear the wine of sediment leaving it bright and fresh.

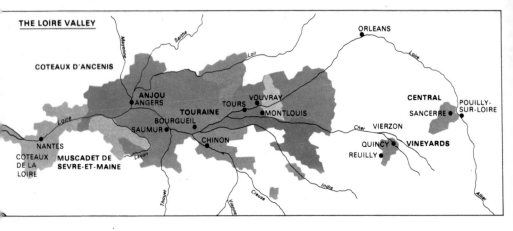

THE LOIRE VALLEY

COTEAUX D'ANCENIS

ORLEANS

ANJOU
ANGERS
TOURAINE
BOURGUEIL
SAUMUR

VOUVRAY
TOURS
MONTLOUIS
CHINON

CENTRAL
SANCERRE
VIERZON
QUINCY
REUILLY

POUILLY-
SUR-LOIRE

NANTES
COTEAUX
DE LA
LOIRE

MUSCADET DE
SEVRE-ET-MAINE

VINEYARDS

The Loire

The Loire, one of the longest and most beautiful rivers in Europe, passes through the oldest civilized region of France, an area of châteaux and castles, frequented for generations by her rulers. Rising on the Cévennes Mountains in the Massif Central, the river winds its way lazily, but sometimes violently, for over 1070 kilometres passing through 15 wine-growing areas before entering the sea in Britanny. These areas have to some extent a common identity in the delicacy of their wines which have a definite family likeness. Even so, by virtue of the great distances they are apart, growers from different regions know little of each other.

Unlike the districts of Bordeaux and Burgundy the area is not commercialized. Until the last 20 years, the wines were drunk mostly locally or in Paris. However, their excellence is now generally acknowledged.

Throughout the 202,000 hectares of vineyards, there is an immense variety of soil, including clay, pebbly gravel, limestone, chalk and marl. As a result, many varieties of grapes are grown to suit the ever changing pattern of land and climate. Cabernet Franc is believed to have come from Bordeaux many centuries ago. It is known as Breton in the Touraine district, where both red and rosé wines are produced in considerable quantities. Chasselas is used for over 70 per cent of the dry, white Pouilly-sur-Loire wines, while Sauvignon Blanc, the white grape from Bordeaux, produces the excellent dry, white wines of Sancerre and Pouilly-Blanc-Fumé. Muscadet, originating from Burgundy in the mid-17th century, produces light, fresh, dry white wines from near the mouth of the Loire, excellent with sea food from Normandy. Chenin Blanc, the oldest and most widely cultivated grape, in the Loire is used for both sweet and dry wines and Cabernet Sauvignon is mostly used in Anjou for rosé.

Pays Nantes

The vineyards at the estuary of the Loire are mainly on the left bank of the river. They produce clean, fresh, dry, white wines, the best of which come from the hillsides. Muscadet, the most important wine, is produced from a vine of the same name round the town of Nantes. The best types—those bearing the appellation Muscadet de Sévre et Maine or Muscadet-Coteaux de la Loire—come from the sandy clay and gravel soil of the surrounding hillsides. After pressing and fermenting in casks, the wine is bottled in the following spring. It should be drunk young and fresh.

▼ The Entonneurs Rabelaisiens of Chinon, Indre-et-Loire, are an organization of growers and shippers who meet regularly to discuss various aspects of the local wine trade, particularly methods of marketing wines.

Anjou

Anjou Saumur produces fine, white wines, and, apart from Champagne, one of the best sparkling wines in France. It likewise produces one of the best rosés, slightly sweet but fragrant and refreshing. Produced from the Groslot and Gamay grapes,

be made up from Chardonnay and Sauvignon grapes.

Some of the best and most sought after wines in the Anjou district come from the Coteaux du Layon, covering nearly 50 kilometres of vineyards on the banks of the Layon river. These are high in alcohol and the best vines are only picked after *Pourriture Noble* has set in. The most famous wine, however, is Quarts de Chaume, a sweet but strong and subtly perfumed wine from near the village of Chaume. In most years, it has an alcoholic content of 13 to 16 per cent. The Coteaux de la Loire and Coteaux de L'Aubance, produce good rosés that average around 10 to 11 per cent of alcohol, losing their characteristic Loire charm and lightness if the alcohol is lighter.

the wine should be drunk within a year of vintage as rosés are best when young and fresh. The Cabernet D'Anjou rosé, made from the Cabernet-Sauvignon grape, has a smaller production, is fuller in colour and sweeter.

Saumur

Saumur, an ex-cavalry garrison town, has an elegant riverside position and magnificent châteaux that produce red, white and rosé wines. They also make pétillant, or slightly sparkling, white wines. The white wines from the district are drier than most in Anjou, being more like those from Touraine. They are made from the Chenin Blanc grape renowned for its longevity. However, up to 20 per cent of the wine can

Touraine

Surrounding the town of Tours is an area of over 6,000 hectares of vineyards that produces red, white and rosé wines as well as excellent sparkling wines. It is a charming part of the Loire where villages top the rising ground, while below are little sandy beaches alongside the river. A short detour up river is the most famous appellation for white wine in Touraine, Vouvray. The vineyards stretch over limestone hillsides planted with the Chenin Blanc vines and cellars are hollowed out of the rocky

escarpments. This medium dry wine develops a fragrant bouquet and delicate flavour when bottled.

The red wines, produced from the Cabernet Franc (locally known as the Breton), are classified under the appellations of Touraine, Bourgueil, Chinon and Saint Nicholas de Bourgueil.

Pouilly-sur-Loire and Sancerre

Sometimes known as the Central Vineyards, this is an area of white-wine vineyards on either side of the Loire in central France.

▲ Although mechanization has taken hold in some vineyard areas, particularly in the Midi, many of the old traditions linger on. Here in the Loire Valley a horse is still used to draw a plough between the rows of vines.

The climate is more continental, with short, hot summers and long, severe winters, and allows the Sauvignon vine to produce superb white wines from a soil of mostly chalk and clay with a flinty top covering. Whereas in Bordeaux the Sauvignon produces sweet white wine, here on the chalky soils of the Loire hillsides it gives a unique and truly delicious dry wine—the Blanc Fumé.

Across the river, the attractive village and surrounds of Sancerre produce excellent wines with a distinctive dry Sauvignon nose. These are best drunk young so as to enjoy their outstanding freshness and flavour.

Champagne

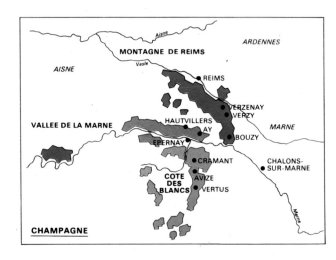

CHAMPAGNE

Why is Champagne the wine of celebration? Because it is something special, fascinating to look at, cheering to drink, a lively, happy wine that just creates happiness? This captivating French wine has been a symbol of perfection and good taste for well over two centuries.

Champagne comes from a carefully de-limited region in northern France round the towns of Reims and Epernay. It covers nearly 30,000 hectares, of which about 18,000 hectares are vineyards, and includes some 250 villages. Consequently, the area covers the majority of the depart-ments of Ardennes, Marne, Aube and Haute-Marne. Both red and white still wines are made but, when not otherwise qualified, the name 'Champagne', in En-glish, only refers to the white or rosé sparkling wine.

The development of Champagne

The sparkling, white wine we know as Champagne dates back to Dom Pérignon (1639–1715), a monk from the Abbey of Hautvillers near Epernay, who began to experiment with the blending of wines of various Champagne vineyards. As cellar master with access to the abbey wines, he was both knowledgeable and enthusiastic, and established that the different areas had individual characteristics, which, when blended together, considerably improved the finished wine. A similar, though no doubt more sophisticated operation, is still carried out by the Champagne Houses to-day. Such was Dom Pérignon's expertise that even when he became·blind, he was still accepted as an expert blender.

He is also credited for introducing the cork to replace the previously used wooden plug wrapped in an oily rag. In this way it was possible to keep the sparkle in the bottle when the wine had its secondary fermentation in spring. However, this raised pressure problems, some merchants losing half their stock due to bottles ex-ploding. The answer was to strengthen the bottles resulting in the special Champagne bottle used today. This is designed to take a pressure of up to six atmospheres (6.33 kilograms per square centimetre).

Increasing popularity

As the art of Champagne production was improved, so the industry grew from around 6.5 million bottles in the mid-19th century to 39 million prior to World War I.

The enormous popularity of Champagne encouraged sparkling-wine production elsewhere in France, some even making their wines by the *Méthode Champenoise*. It must be acknowledged that many are excellent in their own right, and are much cheaper to buy, but they do not have the essential finesse and elegance. Only wines from the delimited area of Champagne, using approved Champagne grapes and made by the *Méthode Champenoise*, can by law be called Champagne.

Vines and viticulture

Champagne is the most northerly Apellation Contrôlée wine-producing area in France with the consequent yearly anxiety as to whether the climate will be friend or foe. The vines are grown on the steep slopes of the chalk hills which in places rise to nearly 275 metres.

French law allows Champagne to be made from only four types of grape: Pinot Noir, Chardonnay, Arbanne and the Petit Meslier. However, less than one per cent of the Arbanne and Petit Meslier are used. The noble Pinot, identical to the grape that produces magnificent red Burgundies in the Côte de Nuits, here gives breeding to sparkling, white Champagne, and is mostly grown round the Montagne de Reims. The Chardonnay, sometimes wrongly referred to as the Pinot Blanc, is grown in the Côtes des Blancs and gives delicacy, freshness and bouquet to the Champagne.

Work in the vineyards is very much the same as elsewhere. Possibly greater care is taken against severe winters and every opportunity is seized to obtain maximum sunshine. The strictest quality control is also exercised at vintage when all imperfect grapes are removed.

▼ The white, chalky soil of the Champagne vineyards imparts the subtle flavour to this great wine.

Classification of quality

This may appear a complicated procedure but it is effective and fair. The vineyards which are small-farmer owned (16,000 owners for 18,000 hectares planted) are classified on a percentage scale as some growers produce better grapes than others. In lesser districts growers are encouraged to plant vines which produce better fruit but less of it, for example white Chardonnay grapes. The rate per kilo is agreed between growers and shippers each autumn and is normally based on the very best growths. This is rated at 100 per cent and the lesser vineyards are then paid in proportion to their rating. Additional premiums are offered to farmer-growers who contract to supply grapes over a number of years.

Vinification and the Méthode Champenoise

The big Champagne Houses press the grapes themselves to ensure their standard is maintained. Only wooden equipment is used as the juice must not be allowed to contact metal.

On arrival at the press-house, the grapes are weighed and then put into the press. This is a simple instrument which takes exactly 4,000 kilograms of grapes (known as a marc) from which the vintner is allowed by law to make 26.66 hectolitres of juice. To get this quantity it is necessary to press the marc several times. Each pressing is kept separate as Champagne of varying quality is produced. The first 20 hectolitres from the marc being known as the vin de cuvée, the next 6.66 hectolitres as the vin de taille. The juice is then rested in casks (débourbage) before the impurities

▶ Cellars beneath Champagne stretch for nearly 200 kilometres. The bottles are stored in *pupitres* during the *remuage* process for the clearing of sediment.

How Champagne is made

▲ The grapes are pressed, the juice fermented and the resulting still wine is carefully blended with others.

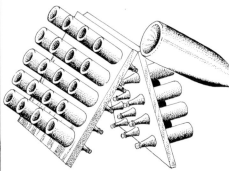

▲ The bottles are placed in special racks called *pupitres* and manipulated daily by hand (*remuage*) so that the sediment moves down the bottle to the cork. Eventually the bottle will be stored neck downwards.

▲ The blended wine is bottled in spring and then undergoes a second fermentation. The bottles are kept on their sides for some years as the wine matures. During the ageing process a sediment forms and this has to be cleared by techniques known as *remuage* and *dégorgement*.

▲ After the removal of the sediment the bottles are dressed for sale.

▲ The sediment is removed by freezing the neck and removing a plug of ice (*dégorgement*). The bottle is topped up with a sugar and wine solution, corked and labelled.

can be racked off and fermentation started.

Ideally fermentation should be carried out with the temperature between 16 and 20°C and the casks must frequently be topped up to prevent bacteria ruining the wine. The resulting still wine is next blended with others in order to produce a wine of consistent quality. Yeasts are added and after bottling and corking, using a cork or crown cork, the wine is placed to rest in deep cellars for a second fermentation. This is best carried out in a temperature of 10 to 12°C and may take up to three

months. The enzymes in the yeasts begin to work on the sugars, but this time the alcohol and carbon dioxide is trapped in the bottle and it is this which gives the wine its sparkling quality. Great wines can be aged for between three and five years, but with the lesser types ageing lasts for about 12 months.

The wine is now 'cloudy' from yeast cells and must be cleared. This is done by placing the bottles at 45° with the necks tilting downwards, in racks called *pupitres*. Each day the *Remueur* shakes the bottles gently and progressively increases the tilt (*remuage*), the objective being to drive the sediment down onto the cork of the up-turned bottle. This normally takes six to eight weeks. *Dégorgement*, or removal of the sediment, is done by freezing the neck of the bottle so producing a small block of ice containing all the fallen sediment. The cork is removed and the plug shoots out. The bottle is then topped up (dosage) with sweetened champagne. The quantity added can vary to produce Champagne to meet the required market: Brut (extremely dry), Extra Sec (Dry), Sec (Medium), Demi-Sec (Medium Sweet), Doux (very sweet). The wine is now given a short rest (*eupilage*) followed by dressing and labelling for the market.

Alsace

It is said that when God made Heaven there was a little over, with which he made Alsace. Scenically and architecturally, this delightful little province, tucked away between the Vosges Mountains and the Rhine, is like a fairy-tale land. Twice in successive wars Alsace has been overrun, but it is now French again. And it says much for the Alsatians' resistance to adversity that it has taken only 30 years to replant practically completely the devastated vineyards and to be awarded an Appellation Contrôlée.

Large vineyards had been established on the foothills of the Vosges Mountains in the 8th century. By the middle of the 16th century, a considerable amount of wine was being produced but under strict production laws, which established grape varieties and the method of pruning etc., with heavy penalties for defaulters. As a guardian of their laws, the Confrérie St Etienne of Alsace came into being and has been their custodian ever since.

The vineyards are still mostly on the slopes of the foothills facing south to south east between about 180 and 365 metres high. They cover over 12,000 hectares and are worked by 35,000 growers. As in

▼ Around the picturesque villages of the lower slopes of the Vosges Mountains, grapes are picked to make Alsatian wines.

Burgundy during the French Revolution, the large estates were split up into small holdings. Today about 50 per cent of the vineyards are less than half a hectare while 75 per cent are less than one hectare.

On the lower ground are orchards which provide the fruit that makes the kirsch, fraise and framboise, so famous in Alsace.

The wine region, consists of two departments—the Haut-Rhin in the south and the Bas-Rhin in the northern sector. The Haut-Rhin, which stretches from Guebwiller to Barr, produces the finest wines in the area.

Climate and soil

The Vosges Mountains act as an important barrier in protecting the Alsatian vineyards from the cold winds and excessive rainfall further to the north. Consequently, the vines enjoy a semi-continental microclimate—sunny, hot and dry, enabling the grapes to ripen to perfection. The southerly aspect of many vineyards means also in a good year, they receive more than 2,000 hours of sunshine, and despite its northern position, the rainfall is only about 600 millimetres per year. Frost and hail, often up to late spring, bring problems for the vigneron. But the danger of frost can be reduced by planting the vines on the slopes and by training them on high trellises about two metres above ground.

Soils can be rich and varied even in the smallest vineyard, so much so that it considerably affects the growth yield and quality of the vines.

Grape varieties

Alsace produces white wines, and unlike elsewhere in France, the wines are known not by the châteaux where they are produced, as in Bordeaux, but by the name of the grape from which the wine is made.

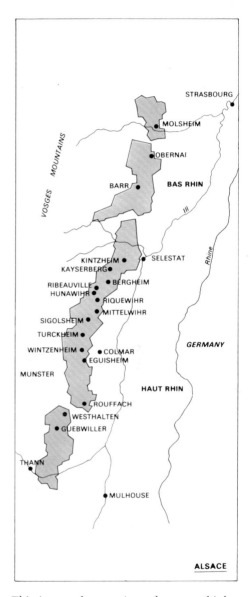

This is sound reasoning when one thinks of the problems the names of some Alsace wine-producing areas could raise if ordering wines of Riquewihr, Eguisheim or Rouffach. Instead these are the much easier grape variety names of Sylvaner, Riesling,

Gewürztraminer, Muscat and Tokay d'Alsace, etc.

Alsace produces some famous white wines, Sylvaner is a soft, light and fruity wine which goes well with fish, shellfish and white meat. Riesling is fairly dry, fruity, tangy and delicate—a classic wine, elegant, with distinction and exquisite flavour. It compliments the finest food, being superb with fish. In contrast, Gewürztraminer, full bodied and luscious, has a spicy flavour and distinguished bouquet.

All these are classified as noble grape varieties, but there are other white wines with controlled names of origin. Muscat d'Alsace is very dry with a characteristic bouquet and taste of fresh fruit, while Pinot Gris is velvety, heady and full bodied, and Pinot Blanc well balanced and supple.

Wine production

Alsace produces about 100 million bottles of wine each year which includes about ten per cent of the AC wines of France. Grower-producers make, sell and bottle around a fifth, while Cooperatives take nearly a third of the production. Producers, besides making their own wine, also buy in from growers. Again Alsace differs from elsewhere in that vintners always buy in grapes, never juice or wine, so enabling them to guarantee what they have bottled. If the word 'Zwicker' appears on the label this indicates a blending of noble and common wines. Alsace wines are bottled in slender flute bottles, a type only used in the region, and should be drunk young and served chilled at a temperature around 7 to 13°C.

Discovering Alsace

The most pleasant way to see Alsace and to appreciate her wines is to follow the 'Wine

▲ Following local custom, the medieval town of Riquewihr celebrates the vintage each year.

Road', a journey through some of what must be the world's most beautiful vineyard areas. The road winds its way through the vineyards along the foothills of the Vosges Mountains, with old medieval ruins among the vines.

There are also some outstanding villages of great historic and scenic interest. For example, Rosheim has fortifications and old Roman houses, and Obernai is noted for houses which date back to the Middle Ages. Dambach has some of the most attractive houses in Alsace with fortified gateways, old walls, narrow streets and ancient wrought iron signs. Riquewihr, virtually untouched since the 16th century, has unforgetably attractive architecture, its houses having carved wooden facades. And Colmar is well known for its gardens, old washing places and the Grünewald Crucifixion.

Côtes du Rhône

It is unfortunate that visitors to France heading to the sea and sunshine of the Côte d'Azur too often speed down the great highway on the left bank of the Rhône with no more than a glimpse at the delightful scenery and fascinating vineyards on the opposite side. For the lover of fine scenery and fine wine, it would be difficult to plan a more congenial holiday than a visit to the Rhône vineyards between Vienne and Avignon.

There is no better place to begin a tour of the northern vineyards than at the world-famous restaurant La Pyramide in Vienne, where the wines of the neighbouring vineyards from across the river can be drunk—reds from the Côte Rôtie, whites from Condrieu.

The Rhône enters France from Lake Geneva in Switzerland and flows between the Massif Central and the Alps. The vineyards of the Côtes du Rhône extend some 200 kilometres, in many places on sheer, high cliffs on both sides of the river. The region has badly defined boundaries, and thousands of hectares of land authorized for vine growing are left unplanted. From an area of around 900 square kilometres, 300 million litres of wine are produced annually. Many of the growers in the Rhône Valley are members of the big co-operatives that receive grapes from the growers and make and sell the wine, paying the farmer-growers from the proceeds. Much of the wine produced in this way is drunk young in cafes throughout France.

In places, the vineyards are on hills so steep that they can only be worked by hand. The soil in general is a well-balanced marl. In the central and northern areas, it becomes a weathered granite, while to the south, round Avignon, there is a predominance of limestone and clay with huge fist-sized boulders.

The vineyards are broken into northern and southern sections by a 70-kilometre, barren strip round Montélimar. The northern part has a continental climate, similar to that of southern Burgundy, with hot summers and temperate winters, while in the southern section, the summers and autumns are very hot with little rainfall.

► Small growers deliver their grapes to a cooperative in the Rhône Valley.

The stony soil reflects the daylight heat from the sun onto the plants. Some heat is absorbed and this is emitted at night, so keeping the plants comparatively warm. Rainfall is mostly in the spring and autumn.

Problems are caused by a strong wind called the Mistral, which throughout the year can blow with great violence from the north. As a barrier against its ferocity, cyprus trees are planted to prevent damage to the vines and other crops which on occasions have been destroyed.

Côte Rôtie

The 'Roasted Slope' is a steep hillside about five kilometres in length and averaging less than a hundred metres wide. The rugged south-east-facing slopes are built up with buttressed terraces, some are so small that they rarely exceed three vines wide and the bushes have to be cultivated by hand. It is on these slopes that Côte Rôtie produces some of the greatest red wine in the Côtes du Rhône. Output, however, is relatively low and even in a good year little more than 1,600 hectolitres are made from Syrah and Viognier grapes.

Condrieu

Condrieu, a downstream neighbour of Côte Rôtie, is situated on the same steep hillside again with numerous stone-retaining buttresses. And like Côte Rôtie, its history goes back to early Roman occupation. Some two dozen owners share about seven hectares planted with the Viognier grape. This produces an attractive, white wine with a distinctive violet perfume. Vinification

◀ A small group of vineyard workers break for well-earned refreshment during the grape harvest. When picking they carry large hods on their backs which take the crop.

varies among the growers to produce wines which range from dry to slightly sweet. Output is limited and in a good year, rarely more than 9,000 litres are made, most of which is drunk in the restaurants of Vienne.

Château-Grillet

Château-Grillet is the smallest vineyard in France to have an Appellation Contrôlée, and it produces the finest, dry white wine in the Rhône Valley. It is just over a hectare in size and under one owner, who produces less than a hundred cases a year from the Viognier grape. This of course brings problems particularly as there is always a demand for this superb wine at the famous restaurants in Vienne where price is no deterrent.

Hermitage

Moving south again and down river is the vine-clad hill of Hermitage towering above the riverside town of Tain. This is another area steeped in history. The vineyard takes its name from a legend that tells how a hermit hid from invading Romans and how wolves and wine-growers from Heaven fed him.

Hermitage, together with the adjoining vineyards of Crozes-Hermitage, Mercurol and Les Chassis, all make good red and

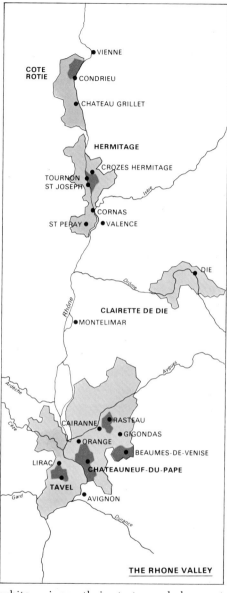

THE RHONE VALLEY

white wines, their taste and bouquet varying with location, sun and vinification. Overall, the area produces more than 900,000 litres each year. Of this, 75 per cent is red wine—rich generous and mellow with a raspberry palate and bouquet. The

61

white wines are dry and pleasantly perfumed with a reputation for longevity.

Cornas and St Peray

These adjoining areas are so much alike in many ways. Cornas has made red wine from the Syrah grape for many centuries. In addition to still wine, St Peray produces the only sparkling wine made by the *Méthode Champenoise* in the Rhône Valley. After the vintage, on the first Sunday in December, a big celebratory wine festival is held, in which everyone takes part.

Châteauneuf-du-Pape

Sixteen kilometres from Avignon on the left bank of the Rhône, Châteauneuf produces one of the Rhône's finest, red wines. Delicate, generous, and very full bodied with considerable bouquet, it is a wine slow to mature and which takes on an 'onion skin' colour with age.

Chateauneuf wines are practically entirely red. A number of grapes are used, the largest proportion being the Grenache. The 'soil' consists of large pudding stones in places more than half a metre deep which, apart from reflecting heat from the sun onto the vines, also absorb and return the heat during the night.

▲ A vineyard in Châteauneuf-du-Pape showing the distinctive pudding stones, the 'soil' from which this incredible wine is produced.

The red wines must have by law a minimum alcoholic strength of 12.5 per cent. Annual production from the 2,400 hectares of vineyards is around 57,500 hectolitres.

Tavel

An area surrounded by sandy, limestone cliffs, Tavel produces the best known of all the great, dry rosé wines. These are full bodied and sturdy, and by law must contain a minimum of 11 per cent alcohol. The vineyards cover in excess of 1,800 hectares and in a good year produce about 22,700 hectolitres of wine.

The Jura

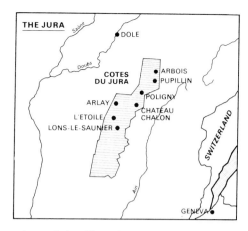

The vineyards of the Jura lie on the foothills of the Jura Mountains, which look out across the Burgundian plains. Hidden away in this quiet corner of France, wine-making has taken place for many centuries. Regretfully, however, very many of the

▼ The buildings of a wine grower in the Jura, an area which produces the famous *vin jaune* or yellow wine. It takes about six years to produce the wine and it is then bottled in special bottles called *clavelins*.

wines of the Côtes du Jura are not obtainable outside France. Other than in Switzerland and Alsace, they are almost sold entirely for local consumption.

The area consists of a wide variety of soils, from pure clay and pebbly marl, to rich limestone. Consequently the vineyards, which cover around 600 hectares produce a variety of wines. Probably the best known of all though are the Rosé d'Arbois and the Château-Chalon. Many wine authorities compare the former very favourably with the much wider known Tavel from the Rhône Valley.

Besides its vin rosé, the Jura produces red, white and sparkling wines. But the speciality of the district is known as vin jaune (yellow wine) or vin de garde (keeping wine). Produced only from the Savagnin grape, this wine is reputed for its longevity —50 years being no exception. Unfortunately, its production is small.

Finally there are vins de paille (straw wines), closely resembling dessert wines, made with grapes dried for three months on beds of straw before vinification and ageing in casks.

Some of the best white wines of the Jura are produced round the small town of Arbois, at Château-Chalon, and the small area of L'Etoile.

Savoie

Surrounded by the foothills of the Alps, the vineyards of Savoie are situated in one of the loveliest parts of France. They produce white wines which are light, fruity and dry, as well as red and rosé wines which are light and tannic, and have a pronounced bouquet.

The area is well known for its many cheeses, in particular, the tomme de Savoie, making an ideal accompaniment to the crisp, white wines of the region. The famous reblochon and the heavier goats' cheeses are better suited with the sturdier red wines of the Rhône valley.

From the southern slopes of Lake Leman near the pretty town of Douvaire comes perhaps the best known wine of Haute-Savoie, namely Crépy. It is a very light, fresh wine, made mainly from the Swiss Chasselas grape, and is often pétillant and

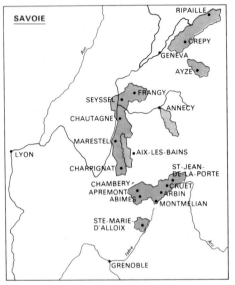

SAVOIE

RIPAILLE
CREPY
GENEVA
AYZE
FRANGY
SEYSSEL
ANNECY
CHAUTAGNE
MARESTEL
AIX-LES-BAINS
LYON
CHARPIGNAT
ST-JEAN-DE-LA-PORTE
CHAMBERY
CRUET
APREMONT
ARBIN
ABIMES
MONTMELIAN
STE-MARIE-D'ALLOIX
GRENOBLE

▼ Grapes awaiting their turn to be taken into the press house. Red and white grapes are sometimes mixed together for production of rosé wines.

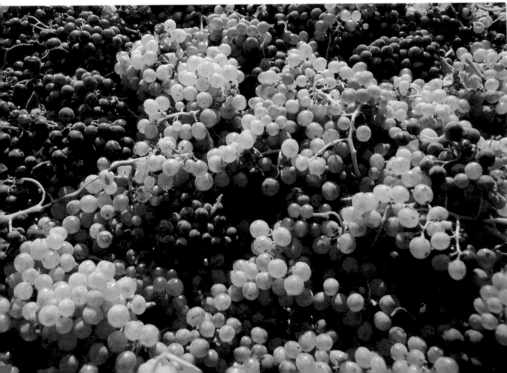

fairly high in alcohol. Crépy is mostly drunk locally.

Another very attractive wine is produced from the vineyards round the town of Seyssel, north of Lake Annecy. Its wines, made mostly from the perfumed Roussette grape are generally lighter and livelier than those from Crépy. Sparkling Seyssel, sometimes made by the *Méthode Champenoise*, though good, lacks quality and is no competition to genuine champagne. Both Crépy and Seyssel have their own Appellation Contrôlée and are the premiers grands crus of Savoie.

Côtes de Provence

Provence lies between the Alps and the Rhône vineyards along the 30-kilometre wide coastal area stretching from Marseille to the border with Italy.

In general, the wines are sound though ordinary, with the rosés accepted as the best produced. These are rather strong with a faint herb flavour. The area produces VDQS wines often sold in special bottles similar in design to the ancient Greek amphorae. Outstanding of the VDQS wines are Côtes du Ventoux, Côtes du Luberon and Côtes du Vivarais.

Only four districts are entitled to Appellations Contrôlée. Bellet, in the mountains behind Nice, produces mostly rosé which is drunk with that great Mediterranean fish delicacy the loup de mer in the hotels in Cannes, Nice and Monte Carlo.

La Palette, unlike the other fine wine areas, is not on the coast. It produces red, white and rosé wines from a number of grapes but chiefly the Grenache. The red wines are rough, while the white are dry and strong. But outstanding are the rosés which are heady with a high degree of alcohol.

The area round the seaport of Cassis produces true pink rosé, claimed by many as the finest and most popular in Provence. The port is noted for its fish and the fine delicate rosé acts as a perfect complement. Bardot also produces excellent rosé wines, second only to those of Cassis, with red and white wines of very good quality as well.

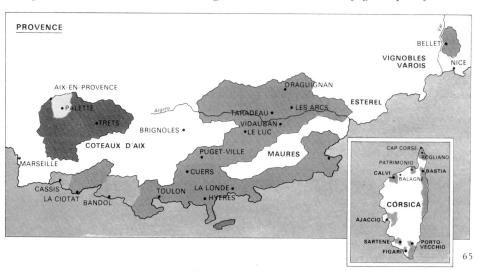

Corsica

The wines of the island of Corsica are heady, strong and high in alcohol. This particularly applies to the big, strong, pink rosés produced near Cap Corse in the northern sector. Corsican wines are drunk mostly in the many restaurants found along the French Riviera.

The Midi

Although most of the major wine-producing areas of France have been covered, there still remains a vast area of land to the west of the Rhône estuary in southern France. The vineyards here account for about a third of the total vineyard area of the country and produce the greatest quantity of vin ordinaire.

Roussillon and Languedoc

Languedoc and Roussillon covers more than 27,000 square kilometres and encompasses the departments of Aude, Gard, Hérault, Lozère and Pyrenées-Orientales. Nearly half the wines of France are produced in this area and apart from a limited number of exceptions all are very much vin ordinaire—the wine that appears on every French table twice daily. There are also 33 defined areas that produce vins de pays and these are spread through all the departments except Lozere.

From the high rugged terrain of the Massif Central, the land drops through hills

and moors to a low coastal plain extending from the Pyrenées-Orientales to the Gard. The vineyards are enormous and vinification is highly industralized with the wine being made in bulk in huge concrete vats holding up to 10,000 hectolitres. There are two principal vines for making red wine. The Grenache has large, soft, oval grapes from which sound supple wine is made, while the smaller berries of the Carignan gives a much tougher wine. White wines are mostly from the Clairette and Ugni Blanc grapes. The Mediterranean climate of hot, dry summers and mild winters enables an average of well over 27 million hectolitres of wine to be produced annually. This vast amount includes over 80 per cent vin de table with little more than three per cent Appellation Contrôlée.

Although the wine is produced in such enormous quantity, there are still individual wines. But none of these has such distinction as the great wines of Burgundy, Bordeaux, Alsace or the Rhône.

Banyuls produces a sweet, natural wine

▶ Vintage at Roussillon. In southern France vast quantities of wine are made with greater use of more modern equipment.

◀ The vineyards of the Languedoc-Roussillon district above the Mediterranean Sea. The climate and rich soil give a bountiful crop although it does not produce great wine.

popular in the area both as a sweet aperitif and as a dessert wine. Muscat de Frontignan, a rich, dark yellow, dessert wine made near Montpellier, has a very marked grapey taste and is an agreeable wine to drink with fruit or a sweet. Corbières Maritimes a deep red wine from near Perpignan, is an ideal accompaniment to the heavily-garlicked cassoulet—a dish most popular in the area. The wine is not unlike Mâcon which with age becomes smooth and pleasant.

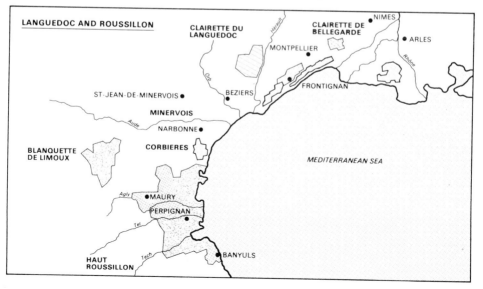

Tasting

Taste is probably one of the most difficult things to describe, and this is no less so for wine. Descriptions used by the wine trade make it no easier and however knowledgeable one is of either wine or the English language it is always difficult to comprehend the jargon used by the professional taster. Rather than trying to understand this extensive and varying vocabulary the following chapter is intended to remove the mystique which can be quite offputting.

The taste of wine in a glass is the result of a complicated interaction of numerous factors.

The chemical and physical properties of the sun affect the chemicals of the grape juice and thus the final taste of the wine even before it is made. Climatic conditions influence the ripeness of the fruit which affects the varying amounts of sugar and acids in the juice. The type of grape used will also have a major bearing on the wine's taste. Some wines are the product of one particular variety while others are blended from the juice of a number of different kinds.

Man, too, with his skill and care during the growing period, supplies the hus-bandry that assists nature to produce the luscious ripe grapes.

It is important to remember that the conditions under which the grapes are grown are not constant from year to year. Consequently there are subtle differences in the wine—some years produce excellent wines while others are not so good. This is the vintage factor which must be taken into account when tasting wines.

Because of the diverse nature of the raw material, the wine-maker can produce wines of various styles and qualities. He can also modify nature's variations, for example, by varying the speed and temperature of the fermentation. And by stopping the fermentation early, he can increase the sugar content of the wine. Maturation can be long or short in either cask or bottle, or even in both.

These and many other techniques are used by the wine merchant to enable him to supply the needs of the consumer, whether he requires a young or old, sweet or dry, red, white or rosé, inexpensive or costly wine.

There are, of course, many things that can happen to a wine during storage and maturation—it can get out of condition. Consequently, quality control in a wine business is a very exacting art and the wine merchant should make sure that all wines are in perfect condition by the time they reach the consumer.

The tasting glass

Sloping sides to concentrate bouquet at mouth of glass

Glass only one third filled to allow wine to breath

Stem to keep heat of hand away from wine

How to taste

Tasting is a three part operation using first the eyes, second the nose and third the palate. It is necessary to learn how to identify wines building up a memory bank of smells and tastes.

ORDER OF TASTING

1. dry wines before sweet wines
2. dry white wines before red wines
3. red wines before sweet white wines
4. young wines before old wines

The eyes

Many judgements can be made by looking at the wine, which should be clear and bright. If there is sediment in it, this should be separated by decanting before the wine is served.

Besides clarity, the eye will give you a lead towards both the style and maturity of the wine in the glass. This therefore, brings us to colour. A white wine can vary from being almost water white, with a pale tinge, through straw colour to a rich golden hue in some luscious wines such as Sauternes. Older whites tend to turn brownish in colour which is not normally a good sign.

Because white wines are usually drunk while they are young, they should generally, with only few exceptions, be straw coloured, bright and clear.

Red wines are mostly a deep red or ruby colour and like white wines should be bright and clear when poured into the glass. Most red or black grapes impart a rather purple hue to the new young wine which fades to a rich ruby colour as it matures.

With further maturation, this ruby colour changes first to garnet, by taking a brownish tinge, then fades to almost a tan colour with great age. Unlike white wines, many of the great reds will age for as much as 20, 30 or 40 years, or even longer.

The nose

The smell, or, as wine mer-

chants delicately describe it, the bouquet is the next stage in the wine tasting technique. Smell and taste are closely linked, and wine is no exception.

The nose should detect first that the wine is clean and does not contain any unnatural smells. Wine should smell fruity or grapey, after all that is what it is made from. Once a nose has been trained, it should be possible to pick out subtle differences which will identify say a Sauternes or a claret.

▲ Tasting is an art and a science and there is no denying the pleasure on the face of this expert.

Taste

The tasting process is finalized in the mouth. The eye will have indicated a certain direction and the nose will also have pre-conditioned our taste. The taste buds in the mouth will then identify the different qualities—sweetness, bitterness and tannin, etc.—so establishing a rounded assessment of the wine.

Selecting and buying wine

Good quality wine is not necessarily expensive and this allows for some experimentation when buying a bottle. Tasting a variety of wines is the only real way of discovering those you enjoy drinking the most. But how do you whittle down the choice to an actual purchase? This chapter outlines some of the factors you should consider from reading a label to storing wines you've bought for future consumption.

SELECTING WINE

France offers a tremendous choice of wines ranging from the inexpensive vins ordinaires on the one hand to the great growths—grands crus—on the other.

Of the 5·9 million hectolitres of wine that on average are produced each year, about 75 per cent is ordinary wine without any quality status. Around five per cent qualifies for VDQS status while Apellation Contrôlée wines—the quality wines produced to specified standards in certain regions —account for about 20 per cent of output.

Because of the seemingly endless choice and the variations in quality together with the considerable range of prices, it is important when selecting and buying wine to be able to read the bottle label which will tell you much about the contents.

Reading the label

Current EEC regulations control the wording of wine labels throughout the Community. This means that it is not only mandatory to include certain necessary information on the label but that it is also required by law in all EEC countries. Of course, this enables people to recognize the same wine equally well say in Britain and Germany as well as France. The only latitude given is in the use of language. For example 'table wine' may appear on a bottle sold in Britain but this would be 'tavelwein' in Germany and 'vin de table' in France.

The EEC requirements are quite specific. For non-

WHAT THE LABEL SHOWS

Trade mark ————————

Vintage ———————— 1975

Name of wine ———————— MACON

Quality status ———————— Appellation Mâcon contrôlée

MIS EN BOUTEILLES PAR

BARTON & GUESTIER

Name and address of bottler ————————

BARTON & GUESTIER — FRANCE
NÉGOCIANTS A BEAUNE (COTE-D'OR)
PRODUCE OF FRANCE

73 cl

Country of origin   Contents

quality wines, the words table wine, the contents in centilitres, the country of origin and the name and address of the bottler all have to appear on the label.

For quality wine, the label must indicate whether it has VDQS status or is an Appellation Contrôlée wine. If the latter, then the region giving it this quality status, for example, Chablis or Sauternes, must also be disclosed. As with lesser wines the contents, country of origin and name and address of the bottler also have to appear.

Besides this mandatory information, other optional information may be shown. This includes the use of trade marks or trade names but only if they are not misleading. For example, the word 'Bone' could not be used as it could be confused with 'Beaune', which is the protected name of a French quality wine. The vintage may also appear on the label as well as phrases such as 'should be served cool'.

When the wording 'mis en bouteilles au château' appears on the label, it indicates that the brand owners guarantee the wine is authentic and untampered with. If the vintage does not come up to the owners standard then it will be disposed of as a regional wine.

Wines for different occasions

Besides the amount of money you wish to spend and interpreting the label to see that the wine is the particular type you want, there are many other factors influencing choice. Not least of these is the use to which the wine will be put. A special occasion might warrant spending more to get a really excellent wine. And here personal taste will dictate what you buy.

If you want an aperitif before a meal, choice will normally be restricted to a dry wine, as dry wines are better for stimulating the appetite rather than sweet wines which tend to do the reverse. Consequently, these are best drunk as dessert wines. However, if the wine is to be drunk with the meal, then it is important to know the menu so you can select wines suitable for accompanying particular dishes (see page 76).

Although there are unwritten 'rules' generally accepted for matching certain wines and foods, these are not compulsory. It cannot be too strongly emphasized that the final choice must be with the drinker to drink what he likes, how and when he likes.

There are, of course, many wines such as Champagne that can be served as an aperitif and throughout the meal.

BUYING WINE

When to buy

Many factors will dictate when you buy wine. If, for instance, you are in a restaurant then this is obviously a time to drink some wine with your meal. Buying for home consumption enables

METHOD OF STORING BOTTLES

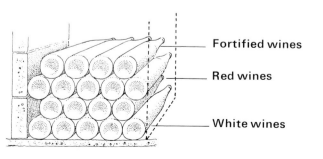

Fortified wines

Red wines

White wines

When storing bottles on top of one another in a cellar, it is a good idea to stack them in a regular order. This will help to maintain the temperature requirements of particular wines. White wines should form the bottom layer as this will be the coldest position, next should come the red, and the top layer should consist of fortified wines such as port and sherry.

you to buy for a specific meal or party, or to accumulate a stock from which you can draw. If you do intend to keep a stock then a suitable storage space is necessary.

Where to buy

The local wine shop or supermarket is ideal if you want wine for immediate consumption or a forthcoming dinner party. And from time to time, they may have special offers of some of your favourite wines. This

▼ Wine racks come in a variety of shapes, sizes and materials. They have a definite advantage over storing bottles on top of one another in that each bottle is individually supported and so can be removed without disturbing any of the others.

again is a good way of building up wine stocks.

Many of the more traditional wine merchants tend to offer 'bin ends' and oddments usually at reduced or favourable prices.

If visiting France, you may get the opportunity of buying local or speciality wines, which may not be available in your local store. These are cheaper than when bought in this country, but the reason for buying them is more likely to be for their speciality rather than the price.

Duty free shops at airports will often save you money on wines although the greatest savings are on brandies and liqueurs for which France is also famous.

For the connoisseur prepared to pay higher prices for some of the older and rarer vintages, there is always the wine auction.

STORING WINE

Once you have bought your wine and you do not intend to drink it immediately, it is important that it is stored correctly. If you are fortunate enough to have a cellar, it is ideal for this purpose although most houses do not have one. In this instance you should take advantage of any part of the house that can simulate cellar conditions. It should be cool and airy with a temperature somewhere between 10 and 15°C. If you are unable to find such conditions, it is unwise to store wine in large quantities but

bulk-buying in, say, dozen lots will certainly save money, so too will buying young wines to lay down.

Storing the bottles

Your cellar, or substitute with suitable conditions, needs to be fitted out so that the bottles can lie on their sides. This will keep the corks moist and the bottles airtight so the wine remains in good condition.

Wine bins or wine racks are ideal for keeping the bottles in the correct position, they can be specially built to fit the required space or bought ready-made. Substitutes such as shelves are only suitable if they are wide enough and sufficiently strong to take bottles. Wine bottles are heavy items so it is unwise to stack too many on top of each other as the bottom ones might collapse.

The cases or cartons in which the bottles are delivered can also be useful for long term storage again if they are strong enough and not stacked too high.

Laying down wines

Although it is advantageous to buy wines while they are young, immature and inexpensive, some expertise is required. In this instance it is probably better to go to a reputable wine merchant who will give you advice on what to buy and when, and how much it is best to take to cover your needs. Some wine merchants will even store the wine for you for a small charge if you do not have your own facilities.

Decanting and serving

In order to get the full enjoyment from wine it ought to be served correctly. Although many people pour directly from the bottle it is still worthwhile decanting. This will prevent any sediment getting into the glass, but more importantly the contact of the wine with oxygen in the air will bring out its otherwise hidden subtleties. Pay heed also to the right serving temperature.

Serving wine at home requires some essential equipment, none of which is expensive to buy.

Basically what you need is a corkscrew and some glasses, but this might be extended to include a decanter and a range of glasses in order to present the wines a little more elegantly.

Corkscrew

As most bottles of wine are sealed with driven corks, the most important piece of

▼ Cork sizes vary according to the quality of the wine. The largest (about 5 cm) is used for fine reds while wines from Bordeaux and Burgundy have corks fractionally shorter. Next down in size, the 4·5-cm cork is used for wines to be drunk early and the cheaper wines have the smallest cork.

equipment to extract them is a corkscrew. These come in many shapes and sizes and usually have one of two types of blade, the worm or the gimlet. It is important to chose one with a worm-type blade as this will give a better bite into the cork. The gimlet type on the other hand tends to tear through the cork especially if the cork is tight.

Place the point of the blade in the centre of the cork, having first wrapped a

cloth round the bottle neck to protect your hand, then twist the worm until almost through the cork and draw it out.

Of all the corkscrews available, the best one to use is the kind illustrated, which has a double spiral action for extracting the cork. The tube is placed round the top of the bottle and the blade wound down. The larger

▲ When removed from the bottle, a Champagne cork should slope outwards at the base (left). If the cork is straight-sided (right) then this suggests that some of the gases from the sparkling wine have escaped.

lever is then rotated and the cork and blade are drawn smoothly from the neck of

DECANTING WINE

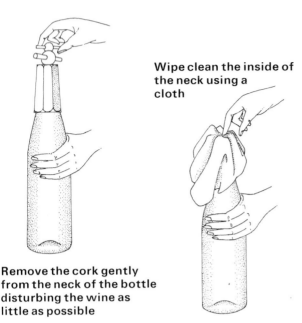

Remove the cork gently from the neck of the bottle disturbing the wine as little as possible

Wipe clean the inside of the neck using a cloth

Pour the wine into the decanter stoppingwhen the sediment reaches the neck. Any wine remaining in the bottle can be poured into a glass and then strained

the bottle. Such a device requires little effort to use and because the bottle is not shaken about then any sediment is not disturbed.

Sparkling wines, such as Champagne, will have the corks wired down because of the pressure in the bottle, and will need a special technique to extract them. Wrap a cloth round the bottle for protection and, making sure that your thumb is on the top of the cork, free the wire from the foil. Then firmly holding the top of the cork, twist the bottle and the cork will slip out without noise or loss of wine.

DECANTING

Most wines are ready to serve straight from the bottle. White wines in particular fall into this category as most are at their best while young and fresh. Red wine on the other hand is usually better if it is aged for a while. This specially applies to the finer more expensive wines, many of which can be in the bottle for 20 or more years. Older wines tend to throw some sediment and the clear bright wine needs to be separated from this before serving.

Preparation and pouring
If you have the wine in your own 'cellar', it will be lying on its side and sediment will have dropped onto the side of the bottle. Carefully remove the bottle in the same position so you don't shake up the sediment and gently take it to where you will do the decanting. If you have

just bought the wine and carried it home, so shaking up the wine, the bottle should be stood upright for at least 24 hours.

Now prepare your decanter. Rinse it first with hot water therefore making sure that it is clean and warm. Extract the cork gently with a double-action corkscrew, keeping the bottle steady, and wipe the inside of the neck to ensure that there are no minute pieces of cork remaining. Then, holding the bottle over a lighted candle so that you can see the sediment rising through the shoulder, pour gently into the decanter. You can, if you wish, use a special decanting funnel which diverts the wine down the inside wall of the decanter. When the sediment rises to the neck of the bottle stop pouring and discard the remaining wine and sediment.

SERVING WINE

Before serving wine it should be brought to the required temperature. Generally speaking most white wines should be served chilled at 13°C, but sparkling wines and sweet wines are better a little cooler at 10°C. This can be attained by placing the wine in a refrigerator for about an hour or in an ice bucket for approximately 20 minutes.

Red wine should be served at room temperature and so should be left in the room in which it is to be served for two to three hours prior to drinking.

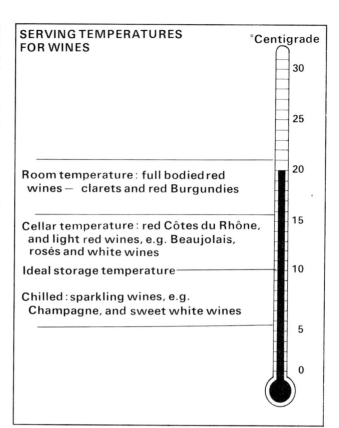

SERVING TEMPERATURES FOR WINES   °Centigrade

Room temperature: full bodied red
wines — clarets and red Burgundies

Cellar temperature: red Côtes du Rhône,
and light red wines, e.g. Beaujolais,
rosés and white wines

Ideal storage temperature

Chilled: sparkling wines, e.g.
Champagne, and sweet white wines

Glasses
Wine will always taste better if served in a thin rather than a thick glass. The glass should also have a stem in order that it can be held without the hand altering the temperature of the wine.

Coloured glass should never be used because it doesn't allow you to see the true colour of the wine. However, it has been used in the past to hide imperfections in the wine.

The best all-purpose glasses are the Paris goblet and tulip glass. The size of the bowl should be sufficiently large to hold the wine and to allow movement within the glass so that the drinker can appreciate the full bouquet or aroma. You will see from this that large glasses are the most desirable. They should never be filled more than two-thirds full and clean glasses should be supplied for each wine.

Special glasses
It will naturally look very much nicer in a table setting if a variety of suitable glasses are used. Traditionally most of the wine-producing regions in France have their own special shaped glass. (See pages 86–87.)

Wine with food

Although immensely enjoyable on its own, wine is most often drunk with a meal. Taste is very much a personal thing and therefore it is not possible to be dogmatic about what wines best complement certain foods. However, this chapter suggests some of the conventional combinations and for those who enjoy cooking it shows how, in a delightful way, wine can also play an integral part in many recipes.

Wine and food accompany each other in a very agreeable way. Most people, however, select the food first then choose the wine. But there is no reason why the food should not be chosen to accompany some special wines. Whatever your choice, both wine and food should be compatible with each other. It is generally accepted that dry, white wine goes well with fish and that red wine goes better with red meat. Here the lighter red wines are more suitable with the lighter meats such as veal, and the fuller red wines are an excellent complement to big red meats such as beef or game. Sweet dessert wines are usually chosen to accompany the sweet course or fruit.

Although these are the accepted combinations ultimately it is a matter of personal taste what wines you drink with particular foods.

There are, of course, a few things which do not accompany any wines satisfactorily. Eggs because of their high sulphur content, are difficult to match with wine. And curries, with their very high spicy content, have a flavour that will kill the taste

of most wines. Pickled or vinegary foods can also make the delicate flavour of wine hard to taste.

Cheese and wine

Most cheeses go extremely well with wine. Again the

same rules apply that do for other foods—the lighter more delicate cheeses should be accompanied by the lighter more delicate wines. Conversely the bigger more robust cheeses should be accompanied by

WINES WITH FOOD	
Food	**Wines**
Fish; oysters; shellfish	Dry white wines; sparkling dry white wine: Brut Champagne
Entrées: hors d'oeuvre	Dry, or medium dry, white wine; rosé
Meat: poultry	Red wines with a rich bouquet
Game	Any of the great red wines that are full bodied, generous and strong
Cheeses: strong mild	Great red wines of good vintage regional white wines
Paté: foie gras	According to preference, great red wines or sweet white wines
Sweet course	Champagne: any other sparkling wine: sweet wines: sweet dessert wines
Fruit	Champagne: sweet white wines
Champagne may be used to accompany any meal	

the heavier more flavour-some wines.

Regional wines with regional foods

In France, because locally produced wines are usually more readily available than those from other regions, there are many very interesting regional recipes which go extremely well with the wines also produced in that region. Numerous cookery books exist to which you can refer for more detailed information.

RECIPES

Below are some easy-to-prepare recipes which involve cooking with wine. It is not necessary to use expensive wines as these are best for drinking with the meal. See page 76 for suggestions on what wines to serve with particular foods.

STARTER:
Scallops with white wine

6 scallops
150 ml ($\frac{1}{4}$ pint) water
few drops lemon juice
30 g (1 oz) butter
1 onion
30 g (1 oz) flour
150 ml ($\frac{1}{4}$ pint) dry white
  wine
4 cooked artichoke hearts
60 ml (4 tablespoons)
  browned breadcrumbs
60 g (2 oz) butter
creamed potato
parsley

Remove the scallops from their shells and wash and dry. Place the scallops, water

and lemon juice in a small pan and poach for 5 minutes. In another pan, melt the butter and sauté the onion for 5 minutes. Mix in the flour and blend in the white wine and liquor from the scallops. Stirring continuously, bring to the boil. Halve the scallops and artichoke hearts and add to the sauce. Simmer for a few minutes. Pipe the potato round the edge of the shells. Divide the scallop mixture between the shells. Toss the breadcrumbs in melted butter and sprinkle over the sauce. Grill until golden brown and serve garnished with parsley.

MAIN COURSES:
Porc à fruit

1$\frac{1}{2}$-kg (1-lb) pork fillet
6 large prunes
6 anchovy fillets
6 blanched almonds
45 g (1$\frac{1}{2}$ oz) butter
30 g (1 oz) flour
300 ml ($\frac{1}{2}$ pint) stock
200 ml ($\frac{1}{3}$ pint) white wine
salt and pepper

Store the prunes after soaking them overnight in tea. Soak the anchovies in milk to remove some of the saltiness, then slit the fillets lengthwise and open out. Wrap each one round a

blanched almond and use to stuff the prunes. Lay the prunes down the length of one side of the pork fillet and fold over and tie firmly with string. Brown the fillet in the butter. Stir in the flour and blend in the stock and wine. Bring to the boil and season. Cover the pan and simmer for 30 minutes. Serve the meat cut in slices.
Serves 4

Boeuf à la bourguignonne

$\frac{3}{4}$ kg (1$\frac{1}{2}$ lb) buttock or
  chuck steak
30 ml (2 tablespoons) oil
1 onion
60 g (2 oz) streaky bacon
15 ml (1 tablespoon) flour
1 clove garlic
300 ml ($\frac{1}{2}$ pint) red wine
200 ml ($\frac{1}{3}$ pint) stock
salt and pepper
bouquet garni
125 g (4 oz) button onions
125 g (4 oz) button
  mushrooms

Cut the beef into cubes and brown in 15 ml (1 tablespoon) of the oil. Place the meat in a casserole. Peel and dice the onion, and cut the bacon into strips. Sauté for 2 minutes and stir in the flour, garlic, stock and seasonings. Bring to the boil and stir into the casserole. Cover and

cook in the oven at 170°C (325°F) Gas 3 for 1½ to 2 hours until tender. After 1 hour's cooking, sauté the skinned button onions in the remaining oil and add to the casserole with the whole mushrooms. Sprinkle with chopped parsley and serve with croutons.
Serves 4

Coq au vin

1 1½-kg (3-lb) roasting chicken
125 g (4 oz) bacon
60 g (2 oz) butter
2 large onions
1 clove garlic
30 g (1 oz) flour
300 ml (½ pint) red wine
200 ml (⅓ pint) stock
salt and pepper
bouquet garni
pinch nutmeg

Joint the chicken. Cut the bacon into strips and place in a saucepan with the butter. Fry the chicken joints until golden brown, remove and place in a casserole. Skin and dice the onions and fry for 5 minutes. Stir in the flour and add the remaining ingredients. Bring to the boil and pour over the chicken. Cover and cook in the oven at 180°C (350°F) Gas 4 for 1 to 1½ hours until tender.

Before serving remove the bouquet garni.
Serves 4

Rognons au vin rouge

2 large onions
125 g (4 oz) butter
12 lamb's kidneys
60 g (2 oz) flour
300 ml (½ pint) red wine
300 ml (½ pint) stock
30 ml (2 tablespoons) tomato purée
salt and pepper
bouquet garni
125 g (4 oz) mushrooms

Peel and chop the onions, then fry in melted butter until golden brown. Wash, skin and core the kidneys. Cut in half and add to the onions, cooking for 8 minutes, stirring occasionally. Stir in the flour and add the remaining ingredients. Bring to the boil and simmer for 10 minutes. Remove the bouquet garni and serve with boiled rice.
Serves 4

SWEET:
Tipsy Cake

Cake:
3 large eggs
125 g (4 oz) caster sugar
45 g (1½ oz) butter
90 g (3 oz) plain flour
Filling:
1 large lemon
60 ml (4 tablespoons) dry white wine
60 g (2 oz) caster sugar
300 ml (½ pint) double cream
125 g (4 oz) strawberries

Place the eggs and sugar in a bowl over a saucepan of hot water and whisk until the mixture thickens and leaves a trail (10 to 15 minutes). Melt the butter in a saucepan and cool. Fold the flour and butter into the egg mixture using a metal spoon. Pour into a greased and floured 18-cm (7-inch) cake tin. Position tin in the centre of oven, pre-heated to 190°C (375°F) Gas 5, for approximately 25 to 35 minutes. Turn out and cool, then cut the cake into six thin layers. To make the filling, put the lemon rind, juice and sugar in a bowl and stir. Pour in the cream and whisk until the mixture is thick. Layer the cake with this mixture spreading a little on top. Slice the strawberries and arrange on top of the cake.

Production of French wines

Area	White	Red	Total (hl)
Bordeaux	1,059,799	2,462,257	3,522,056
South-west	316,369	327,348	643,717
Burgundy	318,024	1,339,487	1,657,511
Rhône Valley and South-east	104,608	2,014,072	2,118,680
Loire Valley	1,084,044	691,816	1,775,860
Champagne	1,547,801	33,504	1,581,305
Corsica	5,763	127,178	132,941
Jura	20,484	19,906	40,390
Alsace	857,036	23,467	880,503
Lanquedoc-Roussillon	561,934	104,225	666,159
Total (hl)	5,875,862	7,143,260	13,019,122

Output can vary considerably from year to year. In 1976, the total quantity of wine produced exceeded 73 million hectolitres, but in 1977 it was only just over 52 million hectolitres. The table gives a breakdown of the production of quality wines (in hectolitres) and is based on 1976 figures. In comparison, 11 million hectolitres of AC wines and 1·9 million hectolitres of VDQS wines were produced in 1977.

Recent vintages

The following vintage charts give a general indication of the quality of wines produced in the major vineyard areas of France from 1960.

Below average	Average	Above average	Below average	Average	Above average
Bordeaux (red)			Bordeaux (white)		
	1960		1960		
		1961			1961
		1962			1962
1963			1963		
	1964		1964		
1965			1965		
		1966		1966	
		1967		1967	
1968			1968		
	1969			1969	
		1970			1970
		1971			1971
1972			1972		
	1973			1973	
	1974			1974	
		1975			1975
	1976			1976	
	1977(?)		1977(?)		

Below average	Average	Above average	Below average	Average	Above average	Below average	Average	Above average
Burgundy (red)			**Burgundy (white)**			**The Rhône**		
1960			1960					
	1961			1961				1961
	1962				1962		1962	
1963			1963					
		1964			1964		1964	
1965			1965			1965		
		1966			1966		1966	
	1967				1967		1967	
1968			1968				1968	
		1969			1969		1969	
	1970				1970			1970
		1971		1971			1971	
	1972		1972			1972		
	1973			1973		1973		
	1974			1974		1974		
		1975			1975	1975		
	1976			1976			1976	
	1977(?)			1977(?)			1977	

Below average	Average	Above average	Below average	Average	Above average
Alsace			**The Loire**		
		1961			
	1964				
1965					
		1966			
		1967	1967		
	1969			1969	
		1970		1970	
		1971		1971	
1972			1972		
		1973			1973
1974				1974	
	1975				1975
	1976			1976	
	1977			1977	

Champagne

Year	Generally declared vintages
1960	Non-vintage
1961	Good. Not outstanding
1962	Very good
1963	Non-vintage
1964	Excellent
1965	Non-vintage
1966	Good
1967	Average
1968	Non-vintage
1969	Very good
1970	Non-vintage

Vineyard classification

Pages 16 to 19 discussed the various classifications of French wines. These tables give a breakdown of some of the categories and the châteaux they encompass.

Les grands vins de Bordeaux

Les crus classés du Médoc 1855

Châteaux	Communes
Premiers crus	
Lafite-Rothschild	Pauillac
Latour	Pauillac
Margaux	Margaux
Haut-Brion*	Pessac
Mouton-Rothschild	Pauillac

*Although Château Haut-Brion is in the commune of Pessac, in the Graves de Bordeaux district, it was included in the 1855 classification of wines of the Médoc.

Deuxièmes crus	
Rauzan-Gassies	Margaux
Rausan-Segla	Margaux
Léoville-Lascases	St Julien
Léoville-Poyferré	St Julien
Léoville-Barton	St Julien
Durfort-Vivens	Margaux
Lascombes	Margaux
Gruaud-Larose	St Julien
Brane-Cantenac	Cantenac
Pichon-Longueville	Pauillac
Pichon-Longueville- Comptesse de Lalande	Pauillac
Ducru-Beaucaillou	St Julien
Cos-d'Estournel	St Estèphe
Montrose	St Estèphe

Troisièmes crus	
Kirwan	Cantenac
d'Issan	Cantenac
Lagrange	St Julien
Langoa	St Julien
Palmer	Cantenac
Cantenac-Brown	Cantenac
Giscours	Labarde
Malescot-St-Exupery	Margaux
Desmirail	Margaux
Marquis d'Alesme-Becker	Margaux
Ferrière	Margaux
La Lagune	Ludon
Calon-Ségur	St Estèphe
Boyd-Cantenac	Cantenac

Quatrièmes crus	
St Pierre-Sevaistre	St Julien
St Pierre Bontemps	St Julien
Branaire-Ducru	St Julien
Talbot	St Julien
Duhart-Milon	Pauillac
Beychevelle	St Julien
Pouget	Cantenac
La Tour-Carnet	St Laurent
Lafon-Rochet	St Estèphe
Le Prieuré-Lichine	Cantenac
Marquis de Terme	Margaux

Cinquièmes crus	
Pontet-Canet	Pauillac
Batailley	Pauillac
Haut-Batailley	Pauillac
Grand-Puy-Lacoste	Pauillac
Grand-Puy-Ducasse	Pauillac
Lynch-Bages	Pauillac
Lynch-Moussas	Pauillac
Mouton-Baron-Philippe	Pauillac
Croizet-Bages	Pauillac
Haut-Bages-Liberal	Pauillac
Pédesclaux	Pauillac
Clerc-Milon-Mondon	Pauillac
Dauzac	Labarde
du Tertre	Arsac
Belgrave	St Laurent
Camensac	St Laurent
Cos-Labory	St Estèphe
Cantermerle	Macau

Les grands vins blancs de Sauternes

Châteaux	Communes
Premier grand cru	
d'Yquem (Marquis de Lur Saluces	Sauternes
Premiers crus	
Guiraud	Sauternes
La Tour Blanche	Bommes
de Rayne-Vigneau	Bommes
Rabaud-Promis	Bommes
Sigalas-Rabaud	Bommes
Lafaurie-Peyraguey	Bommes
Clos Haut-Peyraguey	Bommes
Coutet	Barsac
Climens	Barsac
Suduiraut	Preignac
Rieussec	Fargues

Deuxièmes crus	
d'Arche	Sauternes
d'Arche-Lafaurie	Sauternes
Filhot	Sauternes
Lamothe	Sauternes
Lamothe-Bergey	Sauternes
Myrat	Barsac
Doisy-Daëne	Barsac
Doisy-Vedrines	Barsac
Doisy-Dubroca	Barsac
Suau	Barsac
Broustet	Barsac
Nairac	Barsac
Caillou	Barsac
de Malle	Preignac
Romer	Fargues

La Côte d'Or

Vineyard	Commune

Les grands vins blancs

Vineyard	Commune
Le Montrachet	Chassagne
Chevalier-Montrachet	Puligny
Bâtard-Montrachet	Chassagne
Les Combettes	Puligny
Blagny-Blanc	Puligny
Le Champ-Canet	Puligny
Les Perrières	Meursault
Les Genevrières	Meursault
Les Bouchères	Meursault
Les Charmes	Meursault
La Goutte d'Or	Meursault
Charlemagne	Pernand

Les grands vins rouges

Grands crus	
Romanée-Conti	Vosne-Romanée
Richebourg	Vosne-Romanée
Clos de Vougeot	Vougeot
Chambertin	Gevrey
Close de Bèze	Gevrey
La Tâche	Vosne-Romanée
Les Musigny	Chambolle-Musigny
Romanée-St-Vivant	Vosne-Romanée
Le Corton	Aloxe-Corton
Les Bonnes-Mares	Morey-St-Denis
Clos de Tart	Morey-St-Denis
Clos-du-Roi	Aloxe-Corton
Grand Echezeaux	Flagey

Premiers crus	
Le St Georges	Nuits-St-Georges
Aux Murgers	Nuits-St-Georges
Les Cailles	Nuits-St-Georges
Porrets	Nuits-St-Georges
Pruliers	Nuits-St-Georges
Les Vaucrains	Nuits-St-Georges
Les Beaux Monts	Vosne-Romanée
Les Malconsorts	Vosne-Romanée
Les Angles	Volnay
La Barre	Volnay
Bousse d'Or	Volnay
Caillerets	Volnay
Champans	Volnay
Les Corvées	Prémeaux
Les Didiers	Prémeaux
Les Forêts	Prémeaux
Santenots du Milieu	Meursault
Clos-des-Mouches	Beaune
Les Marconnets	Beaune
Les Grèves	Beaune
Les Fèves	Beaune
La Boudriotte	Chassagne
Clos St-Jean	Chassagne
Les Epenots	Pommard
Les Rugiens-Bas	Pommard
Les Gravières	Santenay
Les Hauts-Jarrons	Sarigny-les-Beaune

Les grands crus classés de St Emilion, 1955

Châteaux

Premiers grands crus classés
Ausone
Cheval Blanc
Beauséjour-Becot
Beauséjour-Duffau-Lagarrose
Bel-air
Canon
Fourtet
Figeac
La Gaffelière-Naudes
Magdelaine
Pavie
Trottevieille

Grands crus classés
l'Arrosée
Clos l'Angélus
Balestard-la-Tonnelle
Bellevue
Bergat
Cadet-Bon
Cadet-Piola
Canon-la-Gaffelière
Cap-de-Mourlin
Chapelle-Madeleine
Chauvin
Corbin
Coutet
Croque-Michotte
Cure-Bon-la-Madeleine
Fonplégade
Fonroque
Franc-Mayne
Grand-Barrail-Lamarzelle-
  Figeac
Grand-Corbin-Despagne

Grand-Mayne
Grand-Pontet
Jean-Faure
Guadet-St-Julien
Clos des Jacobins
La Carte
La Clotte
La Cluzière
La Couspaude
La Dominique
Larcis-Ducasse
La Marzelle
Larmande
Laroze
Lasserre
La Tour-du-Pin-Figeac
  (Bélivier)
La Tour-du-Pin-Figeac
  (Moveix)
La Tour-Figeac
Le Châtelet
La Couvent
Le Prievré-St Emilion
Mauvezin
Moulin-du-Cadet
Pavie-Decesse
Pavie Macquin
Grandes-Murailles
Petit-Faurie-de-Soutard
Ripeau
Sansonnet
St-Georges-Côte-Pavie
Clos St-Martin
Soutard
Tertre-Daugay
Trimoulet
Pavillion-Cadet
Petit-Faurie-de-Souchard
Trois-Moulins
Troplong-Mondot
Villemaurine
Clos La Madeleine

Grands crus de Pomerol

Châteaux
Pétrus
Petit-Village
l'Evangile
Trotanoy
Lafleur
Vieux Château Certan
Gazin
Lafleur-Pétrus

Domaine de l'Eglise
La Conseillante
Certan
Latour-Pomerol
Clinet
l'Eglise-Clinet
Le Gay
Nenin
La Pointe
Moulinet
Clos l'Eglise

Visiting vineyards

There are many ways to see a vineyard, varying from organized tours to a casual visit while holidaying in a wine region.

Organized vineyard tours
Many tour operators advertise short visits to a variety of vineyard areas, such as Champagne, Bordeaux, Alsace and the Rhône. These tours include organized visits with tastings to many of the vineyards and cellars of the producers. And they are usually combined with visits to other places of historical interest or of local beauty, usually leaving evenings free to partake of the local gastronomic and wine specialities in the restaurants of your choice.

Wine tours are perhaps one of the easiest and least expensive ways of seeing how wine is made. They usually take place out of the main holiday season and the price includes the cost of travel and hotel accommodation and is usually less than the air fare to the nearest airport. There are, however, other more luxurious gastronomic wine tours, organized for those who prefer a more detailed approach to the wine and food aspect. A travel agent will advise you on the range and availability of the holidays.

Holidays

Most holidays in France, except those taken in the north, will never be very far from vineyards. If you are interested in wine, it is therefore useful to combine a holiday with visits to the local vineyards and to familiarize yourself with the local wines.

While many vignerons will welcome visitors who turn up at their premises, it is often wise to plan your visit in advance. Much of this can be done on the recommendation of a hotel or tourist office. An introduction from a British wine merchant might also be helpful.

The word 'degustasion' over the door of a wine establishment, indicates that they are willing to give you a tasting of their products, often with the hope that you might buy a few bottles if you like what you taste. Visits to such establishments, as well as to the local wine shops, will often give you a chance to purchase some wines not always readily available outside their place of origin.

Wine Clubs and societies

There are many wine clubs and societies throughout the country run by local enthusiasts. Some firms and staff associations also run their own clubs. At the national level, there is the Wine and Food society, which now has international connections, and also the Society of Bacchus. Most of these groups, from time to time, organize visits to vineyards for their members as well as arranging tastings and lectures. Many adult evening institutes organize wine appreciation classes, which are available to the general public.

Where to buy French wines

Because of the licensing laws in Britain wine can only be sold through licensed outlets. Besides restaurants and wine bars wine may also be bought from wine shops, supermarkets, or from the many wine specialists who cater for the more unusual smaller productions, or the older rarer wines.

For day-to-day drinking, the more ordinary wines are

available in large variety from supermarkets and multiple wine stores.

If you are looking for the more unusual wines, sometimes called the 'little wines of France', or for the more mature vintages and the wines of the great vineyards, then a visit to a family wine merchant or shipper specializing in these varieties will be necessary.

Many of the very large stores such as Harrods and Fortnum and Mason in London, or their equivalents in provincial cities, specialize in always carrying a large variety of French wines.

Some reputable wine companies run wine clubs, offering to their customers mixed cases and special offers from time to time.

Eating and drinking in France

It is well known that the French regard eating and drinking as an important and leisurely affair. French restaurants therefore tend to have larger menus than their English counterparts. This applies to restaurants whether categorized ordinary or superb in the 'guides' such as the Michelin Guide.

French menus are usually offered à la carte or table d'hôte, giving you a free choice from the à la carte section to set menus usually sold in price groupings, i.e. the 20-, 30-, 40-, or 50-franc menu. While offering traditional French

cuisine, most will offer in additional regional specialities.

Wine to accompany the meal will also vary from the carafe red or white and a fullish range of local wines to a smaller range of the well known classic wines such as Bordeaux, Burgundy and Champagne. The five star restaurants or restaurants of local renown will always offer a larger range of both food and wines to suit those wishing to spend a little more.

The French café

The French café will also offer a variety of drinks besides coffee for the thirsty visitor between meals. The range of wines and spirits is considerable and some even offer specialities such as un kir, a Burgundian drink of white wine with a dash of crème de cassis (a blackcurrant liqueur) making a refreshing cool drink on a hot summer's day.

| Bordeaux | Burgundy | Beaujolais | Champagne |

BOTTLE AND GLASS PROFILES

Weights and measures

New EEC regulations have recently amended existing British labelling and weights and measures legislation. Together with metrication, these have brought many changes to the wine trade. At present, bottles can vary from area to area, but for practical purposes six bottles are equivalent to an imperial gallon which makes a case of 12 bottles roughly two imperial gallons.

By 1980, only specific sizes will be approved and the standard bottle will have to contain 70 or 75 centilitres. Other sizes such as 68 and 72 centilitres will be permitted in the meantime, but will be phased out by 1980.

New labelling regulations demand that the volume in centilitres must be on the label.

Bottles and glasses

Many regions have their own distinctive type of bottle. The silhouettes illustrated above show the profile shape of the more important ones. Glasses from which to drink wine also vary in shape. The tulip glass is frequently used for Bordeaux wines and the Paris goblet is a favourite for Burgundies. But because of the excellent shape of both, concentrating the bouquet at the mouth of the glass, they are most suitable for any wine. For the same reasons the best Champagne glasses are the two illustrated. The saucer-shaped glass so often associated with the drink is unsuitable as too much of the sparkling wine is exposed to the air.

Some regions have their own traditional glasses with distinctive shapes. The Anjou glass, for example, has a long, slender stem and a box-shaped bowl with sloping sides. It is an ideal glass from which to drink chilled, white wine as the stem allows the warmth of the hand to be kept well away from the bowl.

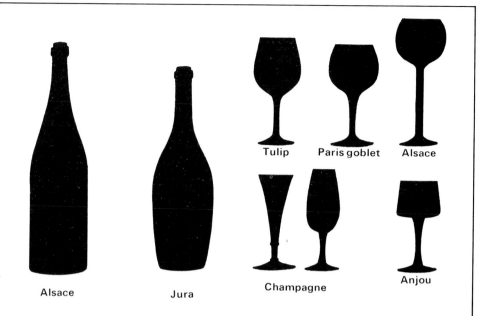

Tulip   Paris goblet   Alsace

Champagne   Anjou

Alsace   Jura

Names and sizes of bottles	
Sizes	**Equivalent in bottles to:**
Quarter bottle	$\frac{1}{4}$
Half bottle	$\frac{1}{2}$
Bottle	1
Litre	$1\frac{1}{4}$
Magnum	2
Double magnum	4
Jeroboam (Champagne)	4
Jeroboam (Bordeaux)	5
Rehoboam	6
Methuselah	8
Salmanazar	12
Nebuchadnezzar	20

Alcoholic strength

Low strength wines, normally are around 10 to 12 per cent of alcohol by volume. In contrast, fortified wines are about 20 per cent with spirits 40 per cent. A simple ratio, 10:20:40, covers the range, with of course, as always, a few exceptions.

Methods of measurement of alcohol vary between countries causing misunderstanding and distrust. The Europeans use a percentage per volume scale (Gay-lussac), while the British use fractions of 175 (Sikes scale) and the Americans fractions of 200. The European system is obviously the most sensible and the one Britain will adopt on 1 January 1979.

Gay-Lussac % by volume	Sikes UK	USA degrees proof
2	3·5	4
4	7	8
6	10·5	12
8	14·0	16
10	17·5	20
12	21	24
14	24·5	28
16	28	32

Book list

The Wines of Bordeaux,
Edmund Penning Rowsell,
Penguin, 1973 75p.
A comprehensive, accurate and
extremely valuable work of the
wines of Bordeaux that will
help both the student of wine
and provide good reading for
the connoisseur.

**Eating and Drinking in
France Today,** Pamela
Vandyke Price, Tom Stacey,
1972.
No longer available from the
publisher, but try your local
library. An invaluable guide to
anyone visiting France—for
both the innocent tourist and
the experienced traveller.

World Atlas of Wine, Hugh
Johnson, Mitchell Beazley,
1977, £13.95.
An attractive, well illustrated
book of all aspects of the wine
trade—comprehensive and
authoritative.

Wines and Spirits, L. W.
Marrison, Penguin, 1970, 40p.
Abounding with information
about the origins and
technicalities of the wine
trade.

**Champagne: The Wine, the
Land and the People,**
Patrick Forbes, Gollancz, 1967,
£4.00.
Possibly the most detailed,
authoritative and entertaining
book ever produced on
Champagne.

The Taste of Wine, Pamela
Vandyke Price, Macdonald
and Jane's, 1975, £5.95.
A highly informative book

which gives a wealth of
information on the appreciation
of wine.

**The Plain Man's Guide to
Wine,** R. Postgate, Michael
Joseph, 1970, £1.50.
An extremely informative book
which is both useful and
detailed.

**France—a Food and Wine
Guide,** Pamela Vandyke
Price, Batsford, 1966.
Out of print but try your local
library. A valuable book for the
gourmet, student and traveller.

**Encyclopaedia of Wines and
Spirits,** Alexis Lichine,
Cassell, 1967, £7.50.
A comprehensive and
authoritative encyclopaedia
which no member of the wine
trade should be without.

A Book of French Wines,
Morton Shand, Cape, 1960,
£2.95.
An old classic, with much to
interest the contemporary
reader. Edited by Cyril Ray.

The Wines of Burgundy,
H. W. Yoxall, Penguin, 1974,
45p.
In addition to wine, contains
useful information for the
traveller.

**Wine Tasting: A Practical
Handbook on Tasting and
Tastings,** Michael Broadbent,
Christie Wine Publications,
1974, £1.25.

Vineyards of France, J. D.
Scott, Hodder & Stoughton.
An interesting, well written
book of the classic areas of
France.

**Alsace and Its Wine
Gardens,** S. F. O. Hallgarten,
Wine and Spirit Publications,
£1.88.

**The Penguin Book of
Wines,** Allan Sichel, Penguin,
1970, 55p.
All about wine, authoritatively
and unpretentiously presented.
Revised and generally updated
by the author's son Peter
Sichel.

Wine, R. S. Don M.W., in the
Teach Yourself Series, English
Universities Press 1968, 55p.
Essential for the beginner.

Winecraft, T. A. Layton,
Harpers, 1935.
This excellent book has been
revised and brought up to date
and provides a valuable
addition to existing
dictionaries of wine.

MAGAZINES

The wine trade has always
been represented by many
magazines, trade papers and
newsletters as well as by many
books. The **Morning
Advertiser** and the
**Scottish Licensed Trade
News** are produced daily.
**Harper's Wine and Spirit
Gazette,** and **Off-Licence
News,** come out weekly. And
**Off-Licence Journal, About
Wine, Ridley's Wine &
Spirit Trade Circular** and
**Wine & Spirit Trade
International** are all
published monthly, while
Wine Magazine is available
every eight weeks.

Glossary

This glossary is intended to provide a ready-reference dictionary of certain terms mostly significant to the world of wine and as used in this book.

Acetic: infected wine tasting of vinegar.

Acid: natural acids are an essential part of sound wine, acting as a preservative and balance. Lack of acidity produces flabbiness, excess will be tart like green apples.

Acidity, volatile: smell and taste of vinegar as a result of over-exposure to air causing the vinegar bacteria to multiply. Must not be confused with fruit acids of fresh white wine. Volatile acids are more pronounced on the nose.

Aroma: impression that a sound wine makes on the nose, relating directly to the smell of the fresh grape from which it was made rather than from any later smell which developed as the wine aged.

Astringency: dry feeling in the mouth, generally on the tongue, caused by a high tannin content in the wine. Normally softens and mellows as the wine develops.

Big: full bodied wine, high in alcohol, flavour, tannin and acidity—mouth filling.

Body: weight of the mouth-filling qualities of the wine, due to alcoholic content and other physical factors brought about by climate, vintage and geographical location, e.g. Châteauneuf-du-Pape compared to northern red wine.

Bottle age: length of time a wine has spent in the bottle.

Bouquet: characteristics, detected by the nose, of the smell developed by the esters and aldehydes from the fruit acids and alcohol.

Carbon dioxide: gas given off as the yeasts convert the grape sugar into alcohol during fermentation.

Chamber: to bring a wine to room temperature.

Collar: to fine, or clarify, a new, young wine in cask.

Corked wine: bottle which is not uncorked (bouché), often wrongly used in the place of 'corky'.

Corky wine (Bouchonné): wine tainted by a foul-smelling or diseased cork.

Crémant: 'creaming'— meaning slightly effervescent (Fr.).

Cru: 'growth' or named vineyard or number of vineyards producing the same quality wines.

Curvée: blend of wines of different vineyards but from the same vintage, or of different years of the same wine.

Dégorgement: removal of yeast sediment from the neck of a bottle of sparkling wine as part of the *Méthode Champenoise*.

Demi-sec: when shown on Champagne labels indicates that the wine is sweet.

Domaine: estate or vineyard.

Egrappoir: rotating cylindrical machine used for removing stalks and for lightly crushing grapes.

Enzymes: proteins that enable certain chemical reactions to take place. An enzyme group known as the Zymase complex is present in the cells of the wine yeast *Saccharomyees ellipsoideus* (the oval shaped fungus that lives on sugar).

Ethyl alcohol: alcohol present in intoxicating drinks as opposed to methol alcohol used in road vehicles.

Extract: soluble solids, other than sugar, which form part of the body and substance of wine.

Fat: big, full-bodied wine with a high amount of glycerine.

Le bon pinard: name for the red vin ordinaire drunk daily with meals in France, mostly from the Languedoc.

Lees: sediment left in the bottom of a cask from newly made wine, normally removed by filtration and racking.

Liqueur de tirage: topping up, after *dégorgement* in Champagne with sugared wine prior to final corking.

Malic acid: fruit acid as found in apples. This is a very acid acid which, round spring time, is attacked by minute organisms which turn it into the much softer lactic acid as found in milk. This is known as malo-lactic fermentation during which carbon dioxide is formed. Too many unripe grapes, can, if untreated, cause a secondary fermentation in the bottle.

Maturation: slow process of subtle chemical changes that eventually bring the wine to its best. Part of the maturation process takes place when the wine is stored in bulk immediately after fermentation and involves reactions with small amounts of oxygen absorbed from the atmosphere. After bottling, reactions that do not involve oxygen predominate.

Must: name given to freshly-pressed grape juice and the wine made before fermentation begins. Though true wine is made from the must of freshly pressed grapes, methods have been available for many years for sterilizing, evaporating or treating it in such a way that fermentation is prevented. Consequently it can be exported as grape juice; such must is used for producing British wine, which is carried out by adding yeast to promote a fermentation.

Noble Rot: see *Pourriture Noble.*

Passe-tous-grains: Burgundian red wine made from a blend of Pinot and Gamay grapes.

Pétillant: crackling or slightly sparkling.

Pourriture Noble: common name for the mould *Botrytis cinerea* that develops on grapes which have been left on the vines after the vintage. The water is allowed to evaporate from the fruit allowing the sugar content to become concentrated, thus giving a flavour of unique richness to the wines made from them. Practised mostly in Sauternes on the Sauvignon and Semillon grapes.

Pulp: solid ingredients left in the must and often chopped up to enable quicker fermentation.

Racking: siphoning wine into clean barrels leaving behind any lees in the old cask. This is carried out after the new wine has been fined to clear it of sediment.

Remuage: process of daily shaking and twisting Champagne bottles so that the sediment slides down the side of the bottle to the cork for removal.

Safrap: lined steel tank designed for carrying about 2,450 litres of wine.

Sec: dry when applied to table wines. A 'sec' Champagne is medium dry, an 'extra sec' is dry, but a 'demi-sec' is medium sweet.

Sorbic Acid: not one of the recognized grape acids, but is sometimes added as a preservative, generally giving off a faint odour of garlic. Its use in Britain, however, is strictly forbidden.

Sulphite: normally in the form of Campden tablets used for sterilization.

Tannin: phenolic chemical substance that helps the keeping properties of wine. This essential preservative comes from the grape skins during the fermentation process though of less importance for white wines for which the skins are removed prior to fermentation. Tannin is broken down during the maturing of the wine.

Tête de Cuvée: best red or white wines from any vineyard in Burgundy.

Ullage: bottle of wine no longer full, due to an old or defective cork having allowed wine to escape.

Vin de Cuvée: Champagne term for wine of the first pressing, i.e. the best.

Vintage: gathering of the grapes. There are wines shipped under the date of their vintage and others without any such date. They differ in that the former, showing promise of improving with age, should be kept while the others are ready for earlier drinking.

Vin ordinaire: wine drunk every day with meals in France —good sound young wine but without great distinction.

Woodiness: smell of good sound oak in a wine. Though unacceptable, it is not unwholesome and can generally be remedied.

Woody: wine that has acquired the smell of the cask in which it has lain too long. A mouldy stave in a cask will give the wine a musty taste, rendering it undrinkable.

Guide to pronunciation

This guide is offered for use where the pronunciation of a French word is not obviously the English rendering. It is hoped linguistically gifted readers will appreciate the reason for its inclusion.

WINES

Claret

Bordeaux Rouge	Borde-doh-Rooj
Bourg	Boorg
Château	Shah-toh
Batailley	Bah-tie-yee
Belgrave	Bell-granve
Calon Segur	Kalahng Saygoor
Chalon	Shah-Long
Clèments	Clay-mong
Ducru Beaucaillou	Doo-Croo Bow-ky-oo
Haut Brion	Oh-Bree-ong
La Mission Haut Brion	Lah mee-see-yong Oh-bree-ong
Latour	Lah-toor
Léoville-Barton	Lay-oh-veel Bahr-tong
Léoville-Poyferré	Lay-oh-veel Pwa-Ferray
Lynch Bages	Leensh-Bahj
Margaux	Mah-goh
Pavie	Pah-vee
Palmer	Pah-mer
Pape Clèment	Pap-Clay-mong
Cantenac	Kong-Ten-Ack
Médoc	Meddoc
Mouton Cadet	Moo-tong Ca-day
Pauillac	Poy-yack
Pomerol	Pom-eh-rawl
St Emilion	Sant Eh-mee-yong
St Estèphe	Sant Eh-Steff
St Julien	Sant Jou-ley-enn

Bordeaux white

Barsac	Bahr-sack
Bordeaux Blanc	Bord-doh Blong
Cérons	Say-rong
Château	Shah-toh
Coutet	Coo-tay
Climens	Clee-mon
d'Yquem	Dee-Kem
Lafaurie Payraguey	La-for-ee Pay-ra-goo-ay
Oliver	Oh-lee-vee-ay
Rieussec	Rwu-sek
Entre-Deux-Mers	Ong-truh de merr
Graves	Grahv
Graves Supérieur	Grahv Soo-pay-ree-ur
Premières Côtes de Bordeaux	Prim-yerr koat de bawr-doh
Ste Croix-du-Mont	Sant Krwah doo Mong
Sauternes	Soh-turn

The Loire

Anjou Rosé	Ong-joo raw-zay
Bourguell	Boor-guh-yee
Château	Shah-toh
de la Bidiere	de lah bee-dee-yer
de Nozet	de noh-zay
Chinon	Shee-nong
Coteaux de Layon	Koh-toh de Lay-ong
Loire	Lwar
Muscadet	Moose-ka-day
Pouilly Blanc Fumé	Poo-wee-yee Blonc Foo May
Quarts de Chaume	Kar-de-Chaume
Sancerre	Song-sehr

Saumur	Sor-moor
Vouvray	Voo-vray

Champagne

Bollinger	Boll-ang-jay
Krug	Kroog
Moët & Chandon	Mow-ett and Shon-dong
Perrier Jouet	Per-ee-ay Joo-ett
Veuve Clicquot	Vuv Clee-koh

Alsace

Alsace	Ahl-sass
Gerwurtztraminer	Gay-vurtz-tram-in-er
Sylvaner	Sill-vaner
Traminer	Tram-in-er

Burgundy red

Aloxe Corton	Ah-lox Kohr-tawn
Beaujolais	Boh-jol-ay
Beaune	Bone
Brouilly	Broo-yee
Chambertin	Shawn-behr-tan
Chambolle-Musigny	Shawm-bohl Moo-seen-yee
Chénas	Shay-nah
Chiroubles	Shee-roo-bluh
Clos de Vougeot	Cloh-de Voo-joh
Côte de Beaune	Coat de Bone
Côte de Beaune Villages	Coat de Bone Veel-ah-j
Côte d'Or	Koht dor
Côte de Nuits	Coat de Nwee
Fleurie	Fle-ree
Gevrey Chambertin	Je-vray Sham-bur-tan
Hospices de Beaune	Aws-peece de Bone
Juliénas	Joo-lee-en-ah
Mâcon Rouge	Mac-ong Rooj
Mâconnais	Makonay
Morey-St-Denis	Mohray-san-den-ee
Morgon	Mawr-gon

Moulin à Vent	Moo-lan ah Vong
Nuits-St-George	Nwee san Zhorzh
Pommard	Pommar
Richebourg	Reesh-boorg
Romanée-Conti	Raw-man-ee Kawn-tee
Volnay	Vawl-nay
Vosne Romanée	Vone Roh-man-ay

Burgundy white

Bâtard Montrachet	Bat-tar Mon-rashay
Chablis	Shab-lee
Chardonnay	Shar-don-ay
Corton Charlemagne	Kawr-tong Shar-le-mong
Meursault	Mirr-soh
Meursault Charmes	Mirr-soh Sharm
Montrachet	Mon-rashay
Pouilly-Fuissé	Pwe-yee Fwee-say
Puligny-Montrachet	Pool-een-yee Mon-rashay

Rhône

Châteauneuf-du-Pape	Shat-oh-nuf-doo-Pap
Condrieu	Kong-dree-ye
Côte du Rhône	Koat-doo-Rawn
Côte Rôtie	Koat-roe-tee
Crozes l'Hermitage	Krows lehr-mee-taj
Tavel Rosé	Tah-vell Roh-say

Jura

Arbois	Ahr bwah
Vin jaune	Van joan

Midi

Corbières	Kohr-bee yer
Muscat de Frontignan	Moc-skat de frong-teen-yong
Languedoc	Long-geh-dock
Midi	Mee-dee

Provence	Praw-vonges
Savoie	Sah-vwah

92

Credits

Artists
Rudolph Britto
Bryan Foster
Sally Launder
David Worth

Photographs
Adespoton: 17, 44
J. Allan Cash: 36
Comité Interprofessional du
  Vins de Champagne: 22,
  26(left), 27(left), 53, 54, 55

The Daily Telegraph/John
  Sims: 8
Robert Estall: 25(bc, br)
Mary Evans: 10, 18
Food from France: 50, 57, 66
French Government Tourist
  Office: 14, 27(right), 43, 58
Robert Harding Associates: 41,
  65
/Robert Cundy: 23
/Denis Hughes-Gilbey:
  26(right), 51, 62, 63
Michael Holford: 6, 9
Moët and Chandon: 19, 30,
  31(left)

The Phillips Collection
  Washington DC: 5
J. F. Sirabella: 31(right), 49
Sopexa: 25(tl, tc, tr, bl), 32, 38
John Topham Picture Library:
  11
/Chapman: 60
/Fotogram: 39, 59, 67
/Geographical Magazine: 46
John Watney: 47, 69

Cover
Design: Barry Kemp
Photograph: Pete Myers